ENGLISH

FOR INTERNATIONAL BUSINESS

ENGLISH

FOR INTERNATIONAL BUSINESS

**Nick Andon and
Seamus O'Riordan**

TEACH YOURSELF BOOKS

For UK order queries: please contact Bookpoint Ltd, 130 Milton Park, Abingdon, Oxon OX14 4TD. Telephone: (44) 01235 827720, Fax: (44) 01235 400454. Lines are open from 9.00–18.00, Monday to Saturday, with a 24-hour message answering service. Email address: orders@bookpoint.co.uk

For U.S.A. order queries: please contact McGraw-Hill Customer Services, P.O. Box 545, Blacklick, OH 43004-0545, U.S.A. Telephone: 1-800-722-4726. Fax: 1-614-755-5645.

For Canada order queries: please contact McGraw-Hill Ryerson Ltd., 300 Water St, Whitby, Ontario L1N 9B6, Canada. Telephone: 905 430 5000. Fax: 905 430 5020.

Long renowned as the authoritative source for self-guided learning – with more than 30 million copies sold worldwide – the *Teach Yourself* series includes over 200 titles in the fields of languages, crafts, hobbies, sports, and other leisure activities.

British Library Cataloguing in Publication Data
A catalogue entry for this title is available from the British Library.

Library of Congress Catalog Card Number: On file

First published in UK 2002 by Hodder Headline Plc, 338 Euston Road, London, NW1 3BH.

First published in US 2002 by Contemporary Books, A division of The McGraw-Hill Companies, 4255 West Touhy Avenue, Lincolnwood (Chicago), Illinois 60646 – 1975 U.S.A.

Typeset by Transet Limited, Coventry, England.
Printed in Great Britain for Hodder & Stoughton Educational, a division of Hodder Headline Plc, 338 Euston Road, London NW1 3BH by Cox & Wyman Ltd, Reading, Berkshire.

Impression number   9 8 7 6 5 4 3 2 1
Year   2006 2005 2004 2003 2002

CONTENTS

ACKNOWLEDGEMENTS

The authors and publishers are grateful to the following for permission to reroduce copyright material in this book:

Unilever.com: 'Unilever Our History' (p. 30); *BBC News Online*: (pp. 32–3) 'Unilever: A company history', 22 February 2000; *Forbes Inc.*: one extract (p. 36) from 'The Super 100' Reprinted by Permission of Forbes Magazine © 2001 Forbes Inc.; *The Economist Newspaper Limited*: one extract (p. 84) from 'Big MacCurrencies' © The Economist Newspaper Limited, London (27 April 2000); *Rebecca Mowling and Associated London Metro Ltd*: (pp. 88–9) 'Two zeros add up to £32 billion loss', Metro, 16 May 2001; *Fiona Joseph and EL Gazette*: for extracts (pp. 115–16) from 'A look at the most effective options available to online advertisers' by Fiona Joseph, June 2001; *BBC News Online*: (pp. 142–3) 'Q&A The Oil Business', 24 March 2000; *BBC News Online*: (pp. 146–7) 'Alternatives to oil', 8 September 2000; *Bill Saunders and the Guardian*: one extract (p. 178) from 'Can an outsider do an insider's job?', 20 March 2000; *BBC News Online*: (pp. 181–2) 'South Korea's top conglomerates present restructuring plans', 14 February 1998.

Every effort has been made to trace and acknowledge ownership of copyright. The publishers will be glad to make suitable arrangements with any copyright holders whom it has not been possible to contact.

INTRODUCTION

Welcome to *Teach Yourself English for International Business!*

This course will give you practice in reading, listening, speaking and writing English in business contexts.

Who is this course for?

It is intended for people who:

- already speak some English but want to improve;
- are working in business and need English for their jobs;
- are studying business and preparing to look for jobs which require English language skills;
- have some knowledge of grammar and vocabulary but are not confident in using their English in real business situations;
- are unable to attend English language classes; OR
- are following a general English course but would like some extra work on business English.

Business is becoming more and more international, and English is an important language, not just to do business in the United States, Britain, Australia and other English-speaking countries, but also as an international language, used when Japanese business people talk to Russian business people, Indonesians to Spanish, Brazilians to Saudi Arabians. In your business career you may find yourself visiting or working in an English-speaking country, working in a company where English is widely spoken, or using English as a medium of communication with other business people from all over the world. You will need to be aware not only of language differences but also of cultural differences that affect the way you talk to people from other countries.

What does the course provide?

The book contains **18 units**, including 3 for checking your progress, plus an **answer key** and a **language reference** section.

The units consist of: **conversations** set in a business context for you to listen to and answer questions about; **articles and reading texts** about business topics; **activities that focus on the language** in the listening and reading texts; activities to practise **speaking** in specific business situations; activities to practise **writing** business letters, e-mails and CVs; **suggestions for further practice** that you can do on your own.

There are also **audio cassettes** or **CDs** to enable you to get the maximum benefit from the course.

How to use the course

Some useful tips for teaching yourself

1 Think about why you are learning English and how you will use your English. Think about the areas you are good at and the things that you are not so good at.

2 Set yourself targets for the week and for the month. Decide how much you are going to study and what you want to achieve in this time. Set realistic targets that you know you will be able to achieve in the time available.

3 Try to set yourself regular times to study each day or each week. A little and often (half an hour a day) is best.

4 When you sit down to study, it is also a good idea to get everything ready. You will probably need a notebook to write answers in, pens and pencils, a small notebook to record new vocabulary, and your dictionary.

5 If at all possible, use the cassettes or CDs. The listening exercises should be done without reading the conversations. You can read them later.

6 After you have done the listening exercises, you can listen to the conversations again. Many people find it useful to listen in the car or when they are travelling on the bus or train.

7 Once you have studied the exercises in the unit, find ways to use them for further practice. Study the vocabulary in the reading texts and use your dictionary to check the words you do not know. Study the pronunciation in the conversations and record yourself speaking.

8 Think about buying a good dictionary and a grammar reference book.

9 Combine the exercises in this book with other ways to practise your English, for example reading newspapers and business journals, writing letters or keeping a diary in English, listening to the News on the TV, watching videos in English, and finding opportunities to speak to people in English. You will find suggestions for extra work at the end of each unit, and in **Taking it Further** at the back of this book.

Using the recording

All the listening passages are recorded onto CD or cassette and are in grey ▇ in the book. If you are studying without these, you can read a written version of the conversations in the book. However, it is much more useful to listen to the conversation without reading the text.

Most listening activities follow this pattern:

1 A **pre-listening activity** to make you think about the topic and prepare you to listen. Sometimes you will be asked to make predictions about what you are going to listen to. In real life this is a good strategy to help you understand and you probably do it all the time without thinking.

2 A **general listening task**. The first task is usually just for general comprehension. The best way to do this is to read the questions before you listen and find the answers while you are listening. Don't worry if you don't understand every word. You don't need to. If you feel unsure about the answers, you can listen again or look in the answer key at the back of the book. However, if you are fairly confident about the answers, go on and do the next listening activity. You can check your answers later.

3 **Listen for the details**. The second listening task is usually more detailed, so you will need to listen again carefully. It is better if you try to do this without reading the written version.

4 **Language exercises** focusing on the vocabulary, grammar and functions in the listening, so that you can study these in the context of the whole conversation.

Here are some other ideas for making use of the recorded conversations:

● You don't need to learn the conversations word for word. However, you could repeat them to practise your pronunciation. It is a good idea to try to make similar conversations adapting the ideas to your own company or your own job.

● Record your own conversation.

● Look up any useful words and expressions that you do not know and make a note of them. (See notes on learning vocabulary below.)

Try to find other opportunities to listen to English, such as the News on the radio or on cable TV. You can also listen to the News via the Internet on websites like BBC Business News. Other ideas include watching English language videos (with the subtitles covered up), attending lectures and talks in English, or taking part in conversations in English with visitors, tourists or just with friends who want to practise their English with you. Don't worry if you don't understand everything, but try to make predictions based on the context, and try to understand the overall meaning before you worry about the details.

Using the reading texts

1 As with listening, before you read, it is a good idea to **make predictions** about what you are going to read. Try to guess from the title what the article is about, and think what you already know about this topic. The pre-reading activities will help you to make predictions and use your background knowledge.

2 The first reading tasks usually expect you to get **a general idea of what the text is about**. This is called "skimming" a text. When you read for the first time, don't worry if you don't understand every word. The important thing is to identify the topic and the main points.

3 When you understand the general idea of the text, you can go back and read again. The second reading task usually helps you to **understand the details** of the text.

4 Now that you understand what the text is about, you can look for new vocabulary and study the grammar that you will find in the reading text. If you don't understand a word, you can try to use the context to guess the meaning.

Some of the reading texts can also be heard on the cassettes/CDs. These texts will contain many new useful words. When you learn the meaning of a new word you should also learn its pronunciation. Remember that we do not always say a word the way it is written. English is not phonetic. Most dictionaries give advice on pronunciation. Listening to these texts may also help you to develop a feeling for the rhythm and music of the English language.

Find things to read outside class. Business newspapers in English contain plenty of interesting business texts. Many English-language newspapers contain a business section. You can also read advertisements, stories, company brochures and business websites.

Learning vocabulary

1 You will come across many new words in this book, and many more if you are finding opportunities to read and listen to English outside the book. It is a good idea to try to guess the meaning:

   a from the context – what is the conversation or article about?

   b from the shape of the word, by analysing its parts, and thinking about similar words you already know. For example, the word *unhelpful* can be recognized easily if you have come across the parts *un-* (meaning *not*), *help*, and *–ful* (meaning the word is an adjective);

   c from what you can work out about its grammar: for example, can you tell if it is a noun, verb, adverb or adjective? If it is a verb, what tense, what is the subject? If it is an adverb, which verb does it tell you about?

2 Use a dictionary. You will probably find it helpful to buy a good dictionary. Very small pocket dictionaries are probably not good enough, as they don't give all the definitions of a word. There are bilingual dictionaries (English–French, English–Japanese, etc.), monolingual dictionaries (English–English with definitions in easy-to-understand language) and specialist business dictionaries. If you are used to working with a computer, there are online dictionaries that you can use on the Internet or purchase on CD.

3 Keep a vocabulary notebook. Note down words with their definitions or translations and write an example sentence. Make sure you review your vocabulary notebook regularly so that you learn the words. Become a word collector and find ways to rearrange your collection to help you remember them.

4 Look for useful expressions as well as single words, and write these down in your notebook as well.

Grammar and functions

The grammar sections in this book only deal with a few key points. We assume that most learners using this book already know the basics of English grammar. However, knowing a rule is not the same as being able to use it consistently without making mistakes.

Try to make a note of grammar rules you are not sure about. The **Language reference** section at the end of this book will help you with some areas of grammar, but you might find it helpful to buy a grammar study book. You can also study grammar online. See recommended websites in **Taking it Further**.

Don't worry too much about grammar mistakes. It is important to be able to understand and communicate. The more you practise, the less often you will make these mistakes.

It can be helpful to think about how you would say the same thing in your own language. If you are aware of the differences, you are more likely to remember the rule in English and less likely to translate word for word.

Writing and Speaking

There are exercises in this book to practise writing and speaking. Sometimes you will just be writing sentences. Other times you will need to write letters or write whole conversations like the ones in the book. This is all valuable practice, so try to find the time to do these longer exercises, even though you may find they take a little time.

Record yourself speaking, if possible with a friend. Then listen to your own conversations and concentrate on areas to improve.

Look for opportunities to talk to or write to people in English. Some suggestions:

a Find a "study buddy" – another person who wants to study English – and try to meet regularly to practise the conversations and situations in the book, as well as ordinary conversations about yourself.

b If you are working in an English-speaking environment, use English as much as possible. Don't worry about making mistakes, grammar will improve with practice.

c Write letters to companies, for example, enquiring about products and services.

d Find pen friends or key pals (e-mail pen friends) and write to them regularly.

Taking it Further

See the suggestions at the end of this book for practising Business English. If you have access to the Internet, this provides many exciting opportunities and we have included a section with useful Web addresses.

Good luck with teaching yourself *Business English!*

1 | COMPANIES

In this unit you will practise:
◆ reading about companies and what they do
◆ understanding descriptions of a company
◆ asking and answering questions about companies
◆ describing the company you work for

Language:
◆ business sectors and activities
◆ word families

Introduction

1.1 *Different kinds of companies*

A Are you working at the moment? Are you looking for a job? Answer these questions about your present company or about the type of company you would like to work for.

- What kind of company is it? What sector is it in (e.g. insurance, shipping, engineering, finance, consultancy, IT)?
- How large is the company? How many employees does it have?
- How many branches (factories, offices) does it have in your country? Does it operate in more than one country? Is it a multinational company?
- How old is your company? When was it founded?
- What exactly does your company do? What services does it provide? If it is a manufacturing company, what does it produce?
- Who are the customers of the business? Who do you sell goods and services to? Other companies? Or do you deal directly with members of the general public?

B   Think of some well-known businesses in your country. Which of these words would you use to describe their activities?

> produces   manufactures   designs   retails   distributes
> provides consultancy services   manages   organizes   imports
> exports   supplies   markets   publishes   trades (in)

Example: *Microsoft designs and manufactures computer software.*

C   Check in a dictionary what these words mean.

Reading 1

1.2 Skim reading – Describing companies

When you read something in English, it is a good idea to **skim read** it first, to get a general idea. Then you can read again more carefully.

- Read quickly
- Don't worry if you don't understand every word
- Look for the key words
- Think about the topic and the main ideas

Now read these descriptions of three businesses quickly to find the answers to these questions.

1 Which company is in the manufacturing sector?
2 What sectors are the other two companies in?
3 Which company is the newest?
4 Which company has the largest number of employees?
5 Which company has offices in the most number of countries?

MULTIMEDIA SOLUTIONS INCORPORATED

At Multimedia Solutions Incorporated we have been designing and managing state-of-the-art commercial websites since 1993. We provide e-commerce solutions for large and small companies in a number of sectors, including business consultancy, travel and tourism and insurance services, from a simple web presence to complete e-commerce solutions.

At present we have over 200 full time Internet consultants and web designers on our permanent staff. Specialist e-commerce teams have wide experience providing consultancy services and setting up and managing sites to meet the requirements of different sectors. We have specialist web design teams working in the following sectors:

- financial services
- insurance brokering and underwriting
- travel services
- computer retailing
- vehicle leasing.

Our head office is in Guildford, near London. We also have offices in Birmingham, Manchester and Edinburgh, as well as agencies in Dublin, Paris, Rome and Madrid.

BENTON INTERNATIONAL POWDERS

Peter Benton founded Benton International Powders Limited in 1979 to manufacture the epoxy resin powder paint he had invented. The powder, when sprayed onto metal and heated in an oven, provides a flexible and durable coating that protects the metal underneath from corrosion. It is used in metal shelving, lampshades, vehicle components, metal garden furniture and thousands of other products.

In the early years it was a very small but profitable business with only six employees working out of a small factory in Surrey. In 1987 International Paints bought shares in the company and invested in its expansion. It is now the largest manufacturer and distributor of industrial powder paints in Europe, and employs 480 staff in six plants in the UK. It exports to 23 countries and last year turnover exceeded £25 million with profits of £4.8 million. Since 1999 the company's head office is in Birmingham near the main factory. The original factory in Surrey is now the site of Benton International Powders' R & D division, one of the world's leading centres of expertise in metalwork paint finishes.

BUSINESS TRAVEL LIMITED

Business Travel Limited is a specialist travel agency providing travel services exclusively for corporate travel. BTL's main office is in London where the company first started up in 1989. It now has 26 offices throughout Europe and in New York and Los Angeles in the United States.

BTL has built up extensive partnerships with a wide range of airlines, hotels and other partners in over 50 countries, and can offer economical travel solutions to large and small businesses. In addition to travel and accommodation arrangements, the company provides a range of services including country briefings before departure and arrangement of meetings and seminars abroad. Major clients include Shell Petroleum, the House of Fraser retail group and IBM (UK) and the company has over 200 travel executives out of a total staff of 270. Last year sales reached £33 million with profits of 1.3 million.

1.3   Read for details – Company profiles

Read the information about the three companies again and fill in the company profile chart below.

Company name	Business Travel Limited		
Main area of business		Website design	
Products / Services			
Customers			
Location: Head office Subsidiaries		Guildford	
When did it start up?			1979
Number of employees			480
Other information			

Language focus

1.4 *Word families*

In English, when you add the suffix *-er* (or sometimes *-or*) to a verb, it usually refers to the person who does that activity, e.g.

to teach   a teacher   to grow   a grower   to act   an actor

Sometimes adding *-er* changes the verb to a noun that describes a tool or machine used to carry out the action:

a cook

a cooker (not the person but the machine used for cooking food)

With certain verbs describing the activities of a company (e.g. *to manufacture, to export, to insure*) adding *-er* (or sometimes *-or*) makes a noun which describes the company rather than the people who work in it.

*Benton International Powders is a paint **manufacturer**.*
*Marks and Spencer is a British clothing **retailer** and **exporter**.*
*VNU, a Dutch company, is the **publisher** of many British magazines including* PC World, Computer Active *and* What PC.
*European Autos is the British **distributor** for BMW & Volkswagen spare parts.*

There are different ways to form the noun that describes an area of business:

*to publish   a publisher   publish**ing***
*Our main business is **publishing** but we are also involved in television and radio.*

*to produce   a producer   produc**tion***
*Ford has stopped **production** of cars in Britain after more than 90 years.*

to manufacture   a manufacturer   manufacture (no change from verb form)
*Ford's plant at Longbridge will in future be used for the **research**, **design** and **manufacture** of diesel engines.*

The table below shows some of the verbs that are used to describe company activities, and the nouns associated with each one.

Verb (describing an activity)	Noun (for the company that is involved in this activity)	Noun (for the activity or sector that a company is involved in)
to manufacture	a manufacturer	manufacture or manufacturing
to produce	a producer	production
to export	an exporter	export
to design	a designer*	design
to distribute	a distributor NB note spelling	distribution
to supply	a supplier	supply
to market	————	marketing
to provide	a provider	provision
to publish	a publisher	publication
to trade	a trader	trade
to organize	an organizer*	organization
to sell	————	sale / sales
to retail	a retailer	retail retailing
to export	an exporter	export
to manage	a manager*	management
to insure	an insurer	insurance
to operate	an operator*	operation

* some of these nouns could also be used to describe a person's job as well as a company's activities.

Practice

A Add some more words to this list.

B Match these well-known company names with their activities in the box on the next page. Use these words in sentences to describe what different companies do.

1 American Express *banking*
2 Amtrak _____
3 AOL Time Warner _____
4 Granada _____

 5 HSBC _____
 6 IBM _____
 7 International Insurers Incorporated _____
 8 Microsoft _____
 9 Nortel Networks _____
 10 Petromin _____
 11 Royal Dutch Shell _____
 12 Saatchi & Saatchi _____
 13 Sony _____
 14 The *Economist* Group _____
 15 Toyota _____
 16 Unilever _____
 17 Walmart _____

---

advertising

information technology

television production and
  broadcasting

food and soap manufacture

oil production

publishing

banking

computer hardware manufacture

motor car manufacture

insurance

hotels and catering

manufacture of consumer
  electronics

operation and management of the
  rail network

broadcasting and internet

design of computer software

electrical and electronics retailer

food retail

1.5 *Vocabulary – Companies*

The following nouns are useful to describe large companies and their parts:

agency	branch	business	company
parent company	department	distribution centre	division
enterprise	factory	firm	head office
headquarters	main office	office	sister company
plant	production facility	multinational	section
subsidiary	warehouse	conglomerate	
group of companies	chain	franchise	

Practice

Group together the words with similar meanings from the list on the previous page:

Example:

  a company   *a business*   *a firm*   *an enterprise*

1 a factory
2 a warehouse
3 a subsidiary
4 the head office
5 a department
6 a multinational

Reading 2

1.6   A group of companies – Kingfisher plc

Complete the description of Kingfisher plc, with one word for each space. You can look at the missing words in the box below, or you can try to complete the description without looking for these words.

Kingfisher plc was (1) _____ in 1983 under the name of Woolworth Holdings, and changed its name to Kingfisher in 1989. It is one of the largest retail (2) _____ in Europe, with over 1,300 stores and over 90,000 (3) _____. Although the Kingfisher group is not so well known, its (4) _____ companies in the UK include famous (5) _____ such as B & Q and Comet. It also (6) _____ stores selling home improvement goods, furniture and tools and electrical (7) _____ across Europe. In addition the group has a presence in Canada, Brazil and China and (8) _____ the Internet.

The Kingfisher retail group concentrates on two main (9) _____ of retailing:

- Home improvement and furniture with the B & Q stores in the UK, Castorama and Brico-Depot in France, and similar (10) _____ in Canada, Poland and Turkey.
- (11) _____ goods, particularly "white goods" such as refrigerators, dishwashers, washing machines, television and audio equipment. Its Comet stores are the second largest electrical retailer in the UK, and in France it is the (12) _____ one electrical retailer with the Darty and BUT chains.

Sales for the Group for the year ending 3 February 2001 were over £12.1 billion, with (13) _____ of over £720 million. The Head (14) _____ for the group is in London.

established	on	groups	office	employees	profits	subsidiary
brands	owns	chains	number	electrical	areas	across	goods

1.7 Describing a company

Choose at least one of the following activities. If you like, you can do more than one, or all three.

A Look at the information about these companies. Write a short profile of one of them for a website, company brochure or newspaper article.

B Look at the information about these companies. Give a short talk about one of them to visitors who have come to find out about the company. If possible, record your talk and listen to it.

C Research your own company or a well known company in your country. Write a short description about the company following the models in this unit.

When you have finished, read/listen to your description, and see if you can improve it.

Chocoholica Limited
Set up in 1990
Main office: Bristol
Branches: London (three shops), Manchester, Edinburgh, Barcelona and Bruges
   217 employees
Area of Business: Manufacture and distribution of chocolates
Products/services: Imports and manufactures luxury chocolates and
                                sweets
                            Wholesale and retail distribution of chocolates
                            Sales of chocolates on the Internet and in own
                                stores
Turnover: £3.7 million in 2000/2001
Profits: £920,000 in 2000/2001

Ryanair

Set up in 1985
Main Office: London
Subsidiary offices: Dublin, Brussels
   1,400 employees
Area of business: Low cost European airline
Products/services: Low cost flights between London, Ireland,
                         Scotland, European and Scandinavian Airports.
                         Internet booking services for over 90% of flight
                         bookings
Turnover in 2000/2001: €487.4m
Profits in 2000/2001: €104.4m

Other information: Now UK's second largest airline, Europe's largest budget airline.
7 million passengers per year over 45 routes across 11 European countries served with a fleet of 31 aircraft.

Reading 3

1.8 *Company organization*

Read this description of the organization and structure of Benton International Powders, which is a subsidiary of International Paints, and find the answer to these questions:

1 How many divisions does the company consist of (in addition to Head Office)?
2 Which division is responsible for transportation?
3 Where are the company's production facilities located?
4 Which division is responsible for quality control?
5 Where is the European Distribution Centre?
6 What functions are carried out in the company's Guildford plant?

Benton International Powders consists of three divisions, Production, Research and Development, and Marketing, plus the Head Office division. Each division is under the overall management of a senior manager who reports directly to the Managing Director.

The Production Division is the largest in terms of numbers of staff, and also in terms of the space it occupies. The Production Manager is based in the Head Office in Birmingham and has overall responsibility for five manufacturing plants, in Birmingham, Leicester, Salford, Glasgow and South East London. In addition, the Logistics Department, which is also part of the Production Division, includes a number of distribution centres, the largest of which is the European Distribution Centre in Faversham, in Kent. The Logistics Department organizes deliveries, supplies of raw materials and stock maintenance.

The Marketing Division is also based in the company's Head Office in Birmingham and employs about 35 staff. The Marketing Division is responsible for advertising and marketing the firm's products, dealing with orders and customer relations and handling customer payments and accounts. These roles involve close co-ordination with the Production Division and the Logistics Department, as well as the Finance Department which is part of Head Office.

The Research and Development Division is based at the company's plant in Guildford in Surrey. That is actually where the firm's original factory was when the business started up in 1979, but now the site is only used for R & D. As well as the development of new products, the Research and Development Division has a quality control function, for example testing samples of paints produced in all the manufacturing plants. The R & D division also provides technical assistance to customers, for example advising on types of paints to use for different purposes, and advising customers about the processes they need to use.

The Company's Head Office, under the Managing Director, has overall control of the company and co-ordinates the other divisions, to make sure that they all work together smoothly. In addition the Finance and Personnel Departments are attached to Head Office and come under the direct control of the Managing Director.

Language focus

1.9 *The organization of a company*

A   Look at this organization chart for Benton International Powders.

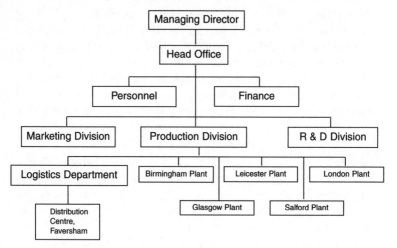

B   Now talk/write about the organization of the company using these expressions:

The company **is divided into** *three divisions.*
              consists of
              is made up of
              is organized into
              has (got)
There are *three divisions in the company.*

The personnel department **is part of** *the company's Head Office.*
                        comes under
                        is under the control of
                        is the responsibility of

The company **owns** *five factories in Great Britain.*
              has got
              has

C   Find the organization chart for your own company, or another company, and write about it in a similar way.

Lesson summary

Here are some of the things you practised in this lesson:

● Vocabulary related to a company's activities:

produces   manufactures   designs   retails   distributes
provides consultancy services   manages   organizes   imports
exports   supplies   markets   publishes   trades (in)

● Nouns and verbs (see **1.4**):

to produce	a producer	production
to export	an exporter	export
to design	a designer	design
to distribute	a distributor	distribution

● Vocabulary for describing large companies (see **1.9**):

head office   a department   an agency   a plant
a distribution centre   sister company

*The company is **divided into** three divisions.*
*Business Travel Limited is **organized into** five regional groups.*
*International Paints **has got** 17 factories throughout the EU.*

*The personnel department is **part of** the company's Head Office.*
*Accounts, sales and payroll are all **under the control of** the finance director.*

Suggestions for further practice

1 Find out more about Kingfisher plc by looking at the company's website: http://www.kingfisher.com

2 Pick a company you have heard of and try to find out the key facts about it. Collect company brochures or find the information in the newspaper, in journals or on the Internet.

3 Look at company profiles (in English if possible) and compare them to the information that you have read in this unit. Do they provide the same kinds of information? How are they different? What else do they tell you? What information do they leave out?

4 Copy the word families from **1.4** into a vocabulary notebook. See if you can add more examples of words that describe business activities. Then think of some more topics for word families (e.g. *jobs* and *occupations*, *travel*, *money* and *finance*) and build up similar tables in your notebook.

5   Choose another exercise from **1.7** or do the same exercise again. It is helpful to repeat tasks and try to do them better each time.

6   Do exercise **C** from **1.9** or one of the exercises from **1.7**, this time using information from a different company.

7   Go through company profiles and look for words you are not familiar with. Try to find groups of words, for example make a list of all the words relating to the different parts of a company (*branch, subsidiary, parent company, head office*) or all the words relating to places and buildings (*site, factory, plant, regional office, distribution centre*) or money and finance (*profit, turnover, income, investment, loan*). Record these groups of words in a vocabulary notebook and learn how to use them.

2 | JOBS AND INTRODUCTIONS

In this unit you will practise:
- ◆ introducing yourself and other people you work with
- ◆ meeting people who work in a company
- ◆ asking and answering questions about jobs

Language:
- ◆ job titles and job descriptions
- ◆ duties and resonsibilities
- ◆ forms of address
- ◆ present simple tense

Introduction

2.1 *Job titles*

Do you have a job at the moment? What is your job title in English? What job would you like to have in the future?

What other job titles do you know in English? How many can you think of? Write a list.

Do activity **A** or **B**.

A Look in an English-language newspaper that has job advertisements, or find a website on the Internet that has job advertisements. (See **Suggestions for further practice** at the end of this unit.) Make a list of job titles. Use a dictionary of business English to find out what they all mean.

B Make a list of business job titles in your own language. You can just do this from memory, or you can look in a newspaper or website in your own language. Then try to translate all the job titles into English. Use a business dictionary to help you.

2.2 *Pre-listening vocabulary*

Match the business cards on the left with the job descriptions on the right.

1

> JB Computers Ltd
> **Mary Black**
> Personnel Manager

a Works closely with a senior executive. Manages the executive's diary, arranges travel and meetings, provides secretarial support such as typing, filing, answering the telephone.

2

> Watermans Books plc
> **Andrew Neill**
> Finance Director

b Is in charge of the arrangements for recruiting new staff, handling employees' problems, managing appraisal and personnel training, dealing with employment problems.

3

> ABC Systems
> **John Smith**
> Managing Director

c Takes overall responsibility for the company's accounts, and controls money coming into and going out of the company. Advises the managing director on decisions related to finance.

4

> Asia Tours
> **Dewi Sutanto**
> PA to the Head of Marketing

d Helps develop the IT skills of employees. Teaches basic PC skills and shows people how to use different software packages.

5

> MRS Industrial
> Machinery
> **Noriko Kensuke**
> Technical Sales Executive

e The head of a company. Makes all the day-to-day decisions about how the company is run.

6

> King's Consultancy Ltd
> **Mohan Singh**
> IT Trainer

f Talks to customers on the phone, arranges sales and delivery of a company's products and services, meets customers to discuss their needs.

Example: 1e

Notice that job titles may be different in Britain and the USA. For example the top executive in a British company is usually called the Managing Director (or MD). In a large US company the equivalent title is Chief Executive Officer (usually shortened to CEO).

Different companies may have different names for the same job, and there are differences between large and small companies and companies in different sectors.

🎧 Listening 1

2.3 Introductions

Jim Smith is being introduced to some of the people who work for Business Travel Limited, a company in London. Listen to the conversations and fill in the missing names and job titles on the organization chart on the next page.

Try to complete this task and the listening questions in **2.4** without reading the text of the conversation. Cover up the text while you are listening.

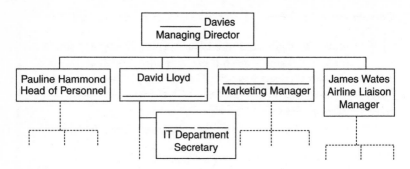

Conversation 1: in the MD's office

GD Come in. Ah, morning Pauline.

PH Hello Graham. Hope I'm not disturbing you.

GD No, I'm expecting a visitor at ten though.

PH I just wanted to introduce you to Jim Smith from the Los Angeles office. He's come over to work on the new Internet project.

GD Ah, yes. Pleased to meet you, Jim. Welcome to London.

JS Thanks very much.

GD You're going to be here for three months, aren't you?

JS That's the plan. I'm really looking forward to spending so much time in England. The longest I've stayed before is a week.

GD I believe we are meeting next week to discuss our plans for the Internet. On Monday, isn't it, Pauline?

PH Yes, that's right.

GD Well, I hope you settle in all right. If there's anything you need, just let Pauline or myself know.

JS Thanks very much.

Conversation 2: in the IT department of BTL

PH David, I'd like you to meet Jim Smith. Jim is co-ordinating the new website project. Jim, this is David Lloyd, he's the IT manager.

JS I think we met last year in New York. At the IT strategy meeting.

DL Yes, I remember. I was very interested in your presentation about new technologies in the travel industry. I'm very glad you agreed to come and work with us.

JS Thanks.

Conversation 3: in the IT department of BTL

PH Jim, this is Janet Andrews. She is David's secretary, and she'll also be looking after you during your stay.

JS Hello Janet.

JA Nice to meet you, Mr Smith.

JS Please, call me Jim.

Conversation 4: in Jim's new office

MH (Knocks on Jim's office door)

JS Come in.

MH Hello. Jim Smith?

JS Yes, that's right.

MH I'm Michael Hopkins. Marketing Manager. I just wanted to say hello and introduce myself.

JS Oh, right, pleased to meet you Michael. I guess we are going to be working together quite a lot.

MH Yes, that's the idea. Anyway, welcome to London. I'll leave you to settle in. Perhaps we can have lunch today or tomorrow.

JS Today would be great. Will you come and get me when you are ready?

MH Of course. At about one o'clock?

JS That's fine. See you then.

MH Okay.

🎧 2.4 *Listen for the details*

Listen to the conversations in **2.3** again.

True or False? Write *T* or *F* next to the statements below to show if they are True or False.

1 Graham Davies has met Jim Smith before. *F*

2 Janet Andrews is the Head of Personnel.

3 David Lloyd already knows Jim Smith.

4 Jim Smith works for an Internet company.

5 Janet Andrews is going to be Jim's secretary.

6 Michael Hopkins is the Marketing Manager of BTL.

7 Michael Hopkins is going to have dinner with Jim Smith.
8 Jim Smith wants Janet to call him by his first name.
9 Pauline introduced the Marketing Manager to Jim.
10 Jim Smith is going to be working in London for about three weeks.

Correct the statements that were false. Rewrite them in your notebook.

Example:

Graham Davies has never met Jim Smith before. OR
Graham Davies is meeting Jim Smith for the first time.

Language focus

2.5 *Forms of address*

Look back at the conversations in **2.3** and answer these questions:

1 How do colleagues address each other at work?
  a Using *Mr/Mrs/Miss/Ms* + first name + second name?
  b Using *Mr/Mrs/Miss/Ms* + second name only?
  c Using first name + second name without *Mr/Mrs/Miss/Ms*?
  d Using first name only?
  e Using second name only?
  f Using their job title?

2 How does Pauline refer to Jim when she introduces him to different people?

3 Is this the same or different in your language?

Generally in Britain and North America people do not use titles (*Mr, Miss, Mrs, Ms*) when talking to colleagues. This reflects an informal working atmosphere between colleagues. However, more junior employees may use titles when addressing a senior colleague, as Janet Andrews did:

Nice to meet you, Mr Smith.
Good morning, Mrs Blackstone.

Even in this case it is normal for people who work together to use first names, so Jim says:

Please, call me Jim.

You would probably only address your boss or a senior colleague as *Sir* in very formal situations. It would be very unusual to address a senior woman colleague as *Madam* or *Ma'am*.

In some languages it is possible to address people by their title (*Herr Direktor, Monsieur le Directeur*). This is not possible in English in business situations.

Reflection and observation

● How is this different from the way you address colleagues in your first language?

● If you work in a company where English is used a lot, make a note of how different people are addressed. How formal or informal is your company?

2.6 *Introducing people*

Here is some useful language for introducing people:

Jim, I'd like you to meet …
I'd like to introduce you to … (more formal)
Peter, this is Jim Smith. (less formal)
Jim Smith, David Lloyd. (less formal)

In business situations, it's normal to say something about the person you are introducing.

Jim, I'd like you to meet Pauline Hammond. Pauline is the head of our Personnel Department.
This is Jim Smith. He's going to be working on the new website.
Jim, this is David Lloyd, the manager of the IT department.
I'd like you to meet Patrick Riordan from British Airways.
This is Sally Ryder, the head of customer relations at …

This is how Michael Hopkins introduced himself:

I'm Michael Hopkins. The Marketing Manager.

Practice

Look at the business cards on the next page. How would you introduce these people to (**a**) the MD of your company? (**b**) a colleague in your office? (**c**) each other?

David Black	**Andrew Jackson**	**Jane Saunders**
IT Manager	*Senior Marketing Manager*	*Finance Director*
Wentworth Travel Ltd	English Petroleum Products	First Class Computers

Jeremy Bowen	**Louise Watkins**
Personnel Assistant	*Payroll Manager*
Pearson-Riley Incorporated	Conway Transport

James Peterson	**Maria Lopez**
Sales Executive	*Customer Care Agent*
Croydon Car Leasing	Thomas Travel & Tours

🎧 Listening 2

2.7 Talking about jobs

Listen to these people talking about their jobs. Then choose the best job title from the list below.

	Job		**Job**
Speaker 1:		Speaker 2:	
Speaker 3:		Speaker 4:	
Speaker 5:		Speaker 6:	
Speaker 7:		Speaker 8:	

a E-commerce co-ordinator   **b** Sales manager
c Secretary   **d** Personnel Manager
e PA to the MD   **f** Receptionist
g Accountant   **h** Finance Manager
i Technician   **j** Sales executive
k External Relations Director   **l** Ticketing agent
m Customer care agent

1 My job is to look after the employees in the company. I am
responsible for recruitment, so if any department needs new staff
my department prepares job advertisements and information about
the post, draws up a shortlist of the best candidates, arranges
interviews and then helps with the interview itself. I also
co-ordinate staff training in the company, and deal with problems
related to pay, pensions, promotion and so on. My department
holds records on every employee in the company and so I have to
make sure that we comply with the Data Protection Act.

2 My job is to work with the sales and marketing departments to
help them develop a strategy for Internet based commerce. We
don't design the company site ourselves, we use an outside
contractor, but obviously I have to work with them to make sure
our website works the way we want it to, and gets maintained and
updated regularly.

3 I'm responsible for sales and so obviously I'm in charge of a
number of salesmen, salespeople I should say. I also help to devise
the company's advertising policy, together with the marketing
department.

4 Well, Charles Hawkson is the Managing Director of the company
and I am his personal assistant. I organize his appointments diary,
make the arrangements for meetings and business trips, answer the
telephone and greet his visitors if they come to see him here. I do
some typing – letters, reports and things like that, but Mr Hawkson
also prepares a lot of documents directly on the computer himself.
I think it's an interesting job because of the variety of things I do.

5 I'm on the front desk, greeting visitors, receiving deliveries, and
also I answer the telephone. It does get pretty busy but there are
usually two of us here.

6 I work under the Finance Manager and basically I keep the
company's books. This means records of sales income,
expenditure, taxes and so on. I'm also in charge of payroll. There
is a payroll clerk who works in the personnel section but I also
have to keep an eye on this area.

7 Well, basically, I sell my company's products. We are a travel company and what we do is sell airline tickets and hotel bookings. We only deal with business travel and the company advertises widely, so basically I am selling our products to people who write in or telephone. Quite a lot of our sales are done with e-mail now, and I think in the future that will become even more important.

8 I do PR for my company, which involves dealing with the press as well as members of the public. We are a large manufacturer of computer peripherals so we do prepare quite a lot of press releases about things that we are doing, new products, special deals and so on. When there are problems we tend to get a lot of enquiries from journalists so I deal with these. Also, major complaints from customers who have some sort of problem, for example if there is a very widespread problem with a particular product line, I get involved in that.

2.8 *Talking about your own job*

Think about your present job, or a job you had in the past, or a job you would like to have in the future.

You are going to practise explaining your job to a visitor or a new colleague.

First, make notes about these things:

- The job title
- The department or section you work in
- Your key responsibilities
- The tasks you do every day
- Who is your manager, and what is your relationship to other people in your department?

Now imagine you are explaining your job to the visitor or a new colleague. What would you say? Write down exactly what you would say and/or practise saying it out loud. If you need help, you can use the framework below or look at the **Lesson Summary** at the end of this unit.

I'm the/a _____

I work in the _____section/department

I'm responsible for _____.

I _____ and _____.

I work under _____.

(I supervise the work of _____.)

(I work with _____.)

Language focus

🎧 2.9 *Job titles*

Look at these words which are often found in job titles:

Senior	Sales	Director
Assistant	Managing	Manager
Vice	Personnel	Assistant
Deputy	Marketing	Accountant
Executive	Human Resources Development	Officer
Personal	Financial	Controller
Chief	Customer Services	Executive
Head of	Accounts	Secretary
Director of	IT	Technician
Assistant to	Public relations	Advisor

These words can be combined in different ways to describe different jobs:

Personal Assistant to the
Managing Director
Senior Sales Executive
Sales Assistant
Customer Services Manager
Director of Financial Services

Customer Accounts Advisor
Personnel Officer
Chief Financial Officer
Head of Human Resources
Development

> Note the use of prepositions:
>
> *PA **to** the Accounts Manager*
> *Head **of** Financial Services*
> *Assistant **to** the Director **of** Marketing and Sales*

🎧 Practice

Put these jumbled-up words back in the right order to make sentences about people's jobs. Check your answers with the recording.

Example: PA the to director I'm
           managing the

I'm the PA to the managing director.

1 head of he's the department the finance   _____
2 an PricewaterhouseCoopers she's with   _____
  accountant   _____
3 Airways from British he's   _____
4 sales department she works of the   _____
  for ICL   _____
5 for they American work in Express   _____
  traveller's division the cheque   _____

Try to find more ways of combining these in job titles. Look at the jobs pages in newspapers or on the Internet and see which combinations you can find.

2.10   *Duties and responsibilities*

Here is some of the language that people use to talk about what they do in their jobs. Notice that the **present simple tense** is used to talk about job responsibilities and duties.

Chief Financial Officer:	*I am in charge of the accounts and finances of the company.*
Personnel Officer:	*I am responsible for recruitment and training of staff.*
IT Manager:	*I run the IT section.*
Head of Sales Department:	*I manage a sales team of 25.*
Customer Relations Officer:	*I deal with customer complaints.*
Secretary:	*I type letters and reports, answer the telephone and organize meetings.*
Purchasing Officer:	*I liaise with our suppliers in different countries.*

Accountant: *I check that invoices are correct, I*
authorize payments and I prepare
account statements for customers.

See **Language Reference** section at the end of the book for notes on present simple tense.

Pronunciation note

Notice that when you use the third person ending, (*-s* or *-es*) the verb sometimes has an extra syllable:

> *manage* (two syllables), *manages* (three syllables), *liaise* (two syllables), *liaises* (three syllables).

1 Find two other verbs in the statements above that add an extra syllable like this.

      _____   _____

2 Practise talking about other people's jobs, like this.
> *The IT Manager runs the IT section.*
> *The Head of the Sales Department manages a sales team of 25.*

Lesson summary

Here are some of the things you practised in this lesson:

● Job titles and responsibilities:
> *Managing Director*
> *Personal Assistant*
> *Personnel Manager*
> *Chief Financial Officer*
> *Sales Executive*
> *Senior Customer Relations Officer*

> *I liaise with airlines and travel companies, and I organize travel and accommodation for business travellers.*
> *Paul is in charge of the IT section and he manages the technicians and IT support staff.*
> *She deals with customer complaints.*
> *They prepare accounts for customers, check invoices and authorize payments.*

● Introducing yourself and other people:
> *Hello, I'm David Haynes, the Director of Marketing.*

This is Pauline Hammond, our Head of Personnel.
David, I'd like you to meet Jane Bruton from KCLE.

● Ways to address colleagues:
Hello, Mike. Morning Jan.
Good morning Mr Matthews. Excuse me, Mrs Baxter.

Suggestions for further practice

1 Research job titles in your company. Find your company's organization chart (or make your own). Find out what the different job titles are and what they mean. Write about some of the jobs in more detail.

2 Imagine you are showing someone around your department. What will they see? Who will they meet? Think of some questions the visitor might ask you about people's jobs. Then practise the dialogue – say it out loud (if you are in a quiet place) or write it.

3 Look for job advertisements in a newspaper (for example the *International Herald Tribune* or the *Financial Times*) or a website that advertises jobs. Make a note of different job titles you find, especially jobs in your own field, or ones that interest you. Note down any information that is provided about the duties and responsibilities of the post. Look up any words that are not clear to you.

4 Look at some business dictionaries and some general English dictionaries and see which one is the most helpful and easiest for you to use. It is a good idea to consider both bilingual dictionaries (e.g. French–English) and monolingual dictionaries (where all the definitions are in English and there are no translations into your first language). Buy a good dictionary and spend a little time learning to use it well.

5 Have you started keeping a notebook of useful vocabulary? You can write down words you find in this book as well as business English words you find for yourself. Organize your vocabulary notebook so that you will remember the meaning of the words and how they are used. Review the words frequently until you have learned them.

6 Do some research on introductions in your company, or any English-speaking company you visit. Notice the way people introduce themselves and others. Make notes about what you have noticed.

7 Think of different situations where you might have to introduce yourself and/or other people. Write some dialogues and practise them.

3 | MULTINATIONAL COMPANIES

In this unit you will practise:
◆ comparing two different accounts of a multinational company
◆ extracting information from tables of company figures

Language:
◆ vocabulary building
◆ word partnerships

Introduction

3.1 *Multinationals and countries*

● Sony, which is based in Japan, and Coca Cola, based in the USA, are companies that operate in many countries. Can you name any other multinationals?

● What do you know about the following companies ? Complete the table using the words in the box below:

	Country	**Business Activity**
Microsoft	*USA*	*computer software*
Volkswagen		
Unilever		
Hitachi		
Barclays		

Countries:	UK Japan Germany UK & Netherlands
Business Activities:	automobiles electronic equipment
	banking household products

🎧 *Reading 1*

3.2 *Skimming and scanning the text*

Unilever is one of the biggest companies in the world. You are going to read an article about its history and development.

1   Which paragraph discusses brands?
2   When did the company begin to sell ice cream?

Unilever has a rich and colourful history spanning more than 70 years

A Unilever was formed in 1930 when the Dutch margarine company Margarine Unie merged with the British manufacturer of soap Lever Brothers. Both companies were competing for the same raw materials, both were involved in large-scale marketing of household products and both used similar distribution channels. Between them, they had operations in over 40 countries. Margarine Unie grew through mergers with other margarine companies in the 1920s. Lever Brothers was founded in 1885 by William Hesketh Lever. Lever established soap factories around the world. In 1917, he began to diversify into foods, acquiring fish, ice cream and canned foods businesses.

B In the thirties, Unilever introduced improved technology to the business. The business grew and new ventures were launched in Latin America. The entrepreneurial spirit of the founders and their caring approach to their employees and their communities remain at the heart of Unilever's business today.

C Unilever NV* and Unilever plc are the parent companies of what is today one of the largest consumer goods businesses in the world. Since 1930, the two companies have operated as one, linked by a series of agreements and shareholders that participate in the prosperity of the whole business. Unilever's corporate centres are in London and Rotterdam.

D Today, Unilever is a supplier of consumer goods in foods, household care and personal product categories. The company also has other operations, mainly plantations in Africa and Malaysia. Famous brands include Dove, Lipton, Magnum ice cream, Omo and Cif.

[*Source:* http://www.unilever.com]

NV (Naamloze venootschap) is Dutch for "Public Limited Company".

3.3 *Understanding text organization*

Choose a heading for each of the four paragraphs in the text from the suggestions below.

Early growth ___   Product range ___
Organization ___   A new company ___

3.4 *Vocabulary*

Choose the best meaning from **a**, **b** and **c** for each word or expression in **3.2**.

1 merged (*line 2*) means   **a** worked closely together
                                     b became one company
                                     c bought

2 distribution channels (*line 5*) **a** ways of getting the product to
       means   the consumer
                                     b ways of finding customers
                                     c ways of contacting suppliers

3 founded (*line 8*) means   **a** discovered
                                     b established
                                     c acquired

4 entrepreneurial spirit (*line 13*) **a** qualities needed for business success
       means   **b** a free spirit
                                          c a sense of responsibility

5 parent companies (*line 16*)   **a** a similar company
       means   **b** family of companies
                                     c principal company within a
                                          group of companies

3.5 *Writing a summary*

The following is a summary of the text in **3.2**. Fill in the missing words. Listen and check your answers on the recording or in the **Answer Key**.

When Margarine Unie and Lever Brothers _____ in 1930 they became a multinational _____ with interests in over 40 countries. The organisation has continued to grow ever since and today is one of the largest _____ _____ businesses in the world. Famous _____ are Lipton, Magnum ice cream and Dove. The headquarters are in _____ and Britain.

🎧 *Reading 2*

3.6 *'Unilever: A Company History'*

Now read a different article about the history of Unilever.

From ice cream to washing powder, Anglo-Dutch group Unilever is one
of the world's biggest makers of household goods. The consumer goods
giant grew out of a merger in 1930 between Dutch margarine company
Margarine Unie and British soapmaker Lever Brothers. Seventy years
later, it has lost out to US rivals Proctor & Gamble and Colgate-Palmolive.   5
Its response to the increased competition is to axe jobs and cull some of
its brands.

The Sunlight company

Lever Brothers was founded in 1885 by William Hesketh Lever with his
brother James. The company produced Sunlight, the world's first   10
packaged, branded laundry soap. Mr Lever established a reputation as
a social reformer, championing a shorter work day, savings plans,
libraries and health benefits. He built Port Sunlight, a tree-lined employee
village outside Liverpool. His empire originally consisted of soap
factories. But in 1917, he decided to diversify into foods. He bought fish,   15
ice cream and canned foods businesses. In 1930, he chose Margarine
Unie as a merger partner. The Dutch company had grown through
mergers with other margarine companies in the 1920s. The logic for the
Anglo-Dutch merger was clear: animal fats were the raw materials for
both margarines and soaps. The new company dabbled in many   20
different areas. During the Second World War it helped make tank
periscopes and soldiers' rations. In the 1950s, it moved into chemicals,
packaging, market research and advertising. By 1980, soap and edible
fats contributed to just 40% of profits, compared with an original 90%.

Persil Power   25

In recent years, the company has faced increasing pressure from US
rivals Proctor & Gamble and Colgate-Palmolive. The launch of Persil
Power was scuppered by the finding that far from cleaning clothes, it
destroyed them. Niall Fitzgerald, who introduced Persil Power, now
heads the company. He got the job as UK chairman in September 1996,   30
when Unilever streamlined its management. Since the mid-1980s, the
company has got rid of its packaging companies, most of its agribusiness
and its speciality chemicals business. This left it with home and personal
care, and foods. The company then embarked on a spending spree in

these three areas. It bought Brooke Bond tea in 1984 and later the 35
Fabergé/Elizabeth Arden brands. Back in the UK, its ice cream brands
– which include Magnum – have been hit by competition investigations.
In 2000, the government called on the three ice cream companies to end
the trading agreements with retailers which abuse their monopoly power.

[*Source:* BBC News Online 'Unilever: A Company History' (22 February 2000)]

3.7 *Vocabulary*

Find the words in the text which have the same meaning as the words
listed below:

1 reduce staff (lines 5–10)
2 basic ingredients (lines 15–20)
3 reason (lines 15–20)
4 became involved (lines 15–20)
5 ruined (lines 25–30)
6 agricultural business (lines 30–35)
7 a period when there was much buying (lines 35–40)

Building your vocabulary

Language learners often try to learn lists of new vocabulary. While this is
useful it can also mean that you have difficulty knowing how to use the
words. Learning "word partnerships" can be helpful. These are two (or
more) word expressions which appear frequently, e.g. *raw materials*,
household products, *parent company*. You will also find it helpful to build
diagrams of word partnerships, for example the word company has many
partners:

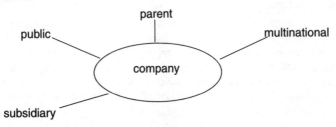

Can you add any more words?

3.8 *Time line*

Complete the time line of Unilever's history:

Year

1885 _____

1917 _____

1930 _____

1950s _____

1980s _____

1984 _____

1996 _____

2000 _____

3.9 *Different types of text*

Below is a list of different types of business publications. Do you read any of them in your work?

- Company annual reports
- Professional journals
- Company newsletters
- Business books
- Business travel guides
- Business newspapers

In which type of publication would you expect to see the following?

---

1 I am delighted to announce that Mr Chris Long has been appointed as the new Head of the Finance Department. Previously, Chris had worked as Assistant Director at Newbolds in the City.

---

2 City analysts were not surprised at today's dramatic announcement of Sir Christopher Blair's resignation. With falling profits and mounting debts, something had to be done to rescue the failing company.

Different approaches

An academic journal and a tabloid newspaper will vary in the way they treat a topic. The audience for the academic text will be scholars and students. The purpose will be to provide an objective and accurate account of a topic. The language will probably be formal. The tabloid newspaper on the other hand will have a mass audience and will want to entertain or persuade its readers. When reading a text ask yourself these two questions:

● Who is the intended audience for this text?
● What is the purpose (to entertain? persuade? inform? etc.)?

Answering these questions will help you to get a better understanding of the text.

Making a comparison

Compare the two histories of Unilever. How do they differ? Think about the following:

● Content: is the text critical/uncritical/trying to persuade/trying to entertain?
● Style: Are there differences in the language, e.g. in the vocabulary?
● Interest: which was more interesting?

Where do you think the texts come from: textbook? official company history? financial magazine? newspaper?

3.10 *Your company history*

Produce a time line for your company. Then write a short history of your company or a company which is well known in your country.

Year ....

....

....

....

....

....

....

....

....

3.11 *The world's biggest companies*

This is a list of the some of the world's biggest companies:

Company	Industry	Country	Revenue ($m)	Net income ($m)	Assets ($m)	Market value ($m)	Employees (000's)
Citigroup	financial services	USA	82,005	9,994	716,937	209,613	173.5
General Electric	electronics	USA	111,630	10,717	405,200	520,686	316.5
Exxon Mobil	energy	USA	160,883	7,910	144,521	290,023	115.0
Bank of America	banking	USA	51,632	7,882	632,574	91,903	163.4
Royal Dutch Shell	energy	Holland	105,366	8,584	113,883	224,265	99.0
Ford	automobiles	USA	162,558	7,237	276,229	59,344	364.6
HSBC	banking	UK	39,348	5,408	569,139	94,105	146.9
General Motors	automobiles	USA	176,558	6,002	274,730	57,498	392.0
IBM	computer systems	USA	87,548	7,712	87,495	190,359	299.2
American Int'l Group	insurance	USA	40,656	5,055	268,238	173,503	52.3
Toyota Motor	automobiles	Japan	120,697	3,812	149,309	170,080	214.6
Wal-Mart	retailing	USA	165,013	5,575	70,245	258,963	1,025.0
Unilever	household goods	Holland	41,418	2,801	26,773	48,462	255.0

[Reprinted by Permission of Forbes Magazine © 2001 Forbes Inc.]

3.12 *Comprehension – check your understanding*

1 Match the terms and the definitions:

    a revenue   **i** anything of value belonging to a company

    b net income   **ii** the amount left after payment of all expenses and taxes

    c assets   **iii** how much it would be worth if sold

    d market value **iv** all the money received by a company/person during a specific period (also known as earnings)

2 Which company has the largest
   a revenue?
   b net income?
   c assets?
   d market value?
   e number of employees?

3 How many countries are represented in this table?

4 Does the list include any IT companies?

5 What kind of companies appear most often in the list?

6 Fill in the gaps in the report below. Listen to the recording to check your answers.
   a There are _____ banking companies in the list. HSBC is from the _____ and the Bank of America is obviously from the United States. The figure for revenues from Bank of America, _____, is greater than the figure for HSBC, $39,348m. However, the _____ of HSBC, $94,105m, is greater than that of the Bank of America, $91,903m.

   b Write a similar paragraph comparing the two energy companies in the list.

Suggestions for further practice

1 You can read more about Unilever at the company's website: http://www.unilever.com

2 You can read more about the world's biggest companies at http://www.forbes.com

4 JOB HUNTING

In this unit you will practise:
◆ understanding job advertisements
◆ talking about qualifications and experience
◆ keeping a conversation going
◆ the layout of a business letter
◆ talking about simple problems and suggestions

Language:
◆ qualifications and skills
◆ work and study experience
◆ beginning and ending a business letter
◆ present perfect or simple past tense

Introduction

4.1 *Looking for a job*

● Do you have a job at the moment? How did you find out about your job? Did you see it advertised? Where? In a newspaper or magazine? On a noticeboard? Did you hear about it from a friend? Or was it advertised on the TV or the radio?

● Are you looking for a job at the moment? Are you planning to start looking for a new job in the near future? What is the best place to find out about the kind of jobs you are interested in?

● Think about your present job, or, if you have not yet started working, ask a friend who has a job in business. Which of these things did you have to do to get your present job?

1 Telephone or send a letter/e-mail asking for further information.
2 Write a letter of application.
3 Fill in an application form.
4 Prepare a CV or résumé.
5 Telephone to arrange an interview appointment.
6 Attend an interview.
7 Do a test.

Which of these could you do in English?

Reading 1

4.2 *Job advertisements*

A Look at the job advertisements on page 40 and make a list of the different job titles. There are six jobs.

1 _____   4 _____
2 _____   5 _____
3 _____   6 _____

B Think about the jobs that are advertised. Which one looks most interesting to you? Why?

C Which job would you **least** like? Why?

4.3 *Comprehension*

Scan the advertisements on page 40. Which one(s)

a require a driving licence? ___
b state the exact salary? ___
c want you to send your CV? ___
d expect you to fill in an application form? ___
e do not give a postal address? ___
f ask for references? ___
g require English plus another language? ___
h specifically mention a university degree? ___
i require some other professional qualification? ___
j offer more information on the Internet? ___
k involve using computers? ___

1

Bilingual executive assistant needed. Must be efficient and well organized with fluent Spanish and English, good computing skills. US $2,500 a month.

Send a letter of application and CV to:

Personnel Department
International Insurance SA
C/Villanueva 29
28001 Madrid

4

ELNET ESPAÑA

Head of Marketing

We are looking for a dynamic, experienced marketing manager to develop the customer base for our Internet and Telecoms services.

For further details and an application form contact:

Srta Martha Caballero
Directora de Selección
ELNET ESPAÑA
Pº de la Castellana, 7–2a
28046 MADRID

2

Accountancy clerk required for expanding business and language training institute in city centre.

We are looking for a qualified accounts clerk/book-keeper who is able to handle student fees and staff salaries. Good English and Spanish. Familiarity with computerized accounts.

Certificate in book-keeping level 3 or equivalent.

Please send CV and the names and addresses of 2 referees to:

USA College of English & Business

Paseo de Gracia 116 bis 28078 Barcelona

3

Business Graduates

We are a large financial consultancy agency looking to recruit between 50 and 100 executive trainees for posts throughout our European network. After initial training, successful applicants will be based in one of our regional offices, providing financial consultancy and planning advice on products including pensions, life assurance, savings, investments and taxes.

Good package plus incentives. Interested?

Phone 01723 590 8080 or e-mail personnel@fse.com

FINANCIAL SERVICES EUROPE

5

Sales Executives

An established mail order and e-commerce retailer with branches in the UK and France is looking for sales executives to help us expand our presence in Spain. No experience necessary, training will be given. Reasonable salary + excellent commission. Interested? Write to:

Telemall International SA
119 Paseo de la Castellana
28046 MADRID

Or visit our website to apply online:
www.telemall.com.es/recruit/salesexec.htm

6

SOFTWARE SUPPORT MANAGER

ICS Ltd provides technical support and training to leading organizations throughout Europe.

We are seeking an experienced IT manager to run a team of 25+ software support specialists working in a major Spanish bank. The post is based in Madrid but will involve some travel within the country.

The successful applicant will have excellent knowledge of a wide range of systems and applications, good Spanish and English, excellent team management skills and the ability to deal with senior managers in our client's organization.

In return we offer an excellent salary + car and other benefits. Apply to:

David James, ICS Ltd, Waterloo Building, Stamford Street, London SE9 1NN
E-mail djames@ics.com, fax +44-20-8747 1357

🎧 *Listening 1*

4.4 *Well qualified for the job?*

Find jobs for these people. Listen to what they say about their qualifications and experience and choose the best job from the advertisements on the previous page for each person.

a My name is Patrick Kiely and I come from Dublin in Ireland. I'm 24 years old. I studied IT and business administration at Dorset College of Further Education. I speak fluent Spanish and reasonably good French. I worked in a bank in Dublin for two years but I gave that up six months ago when my girlfriend moved back to Spain. I have excellent IT skills, but I don't want to spend the whole day in front of a computer screen. I prefer people to computers. I've been living in Madrid for the last six months but I don't have a job at the moment.

b Hello, my name is Teresa Soliz. I'm a secretary. I'm 28. I've had several short-term jobs in Madrid, and London where I lived for two years. I have been working as the Personal Assistant to the director of a real estate company for the last three years, but I would like to change my job and if possible get out of secretarial work completely.

c Hi, my name is Miriam Jax, I'm 35 and I have a degree in international marketing from the University of Mainz, my hometown in Germany. I have worked in marketing for 13 years, in Germany, the USA and Argentina. My present job, which I have had for three years, is marketing manager of a software company based in Madrid.

d My name is Michel Delain and I'm 26 years old. I studied accounts and book-keeping at a private college in France and for the last 18 months I have been working in the accountancy department of a travel company in Bilbao, Northern Spain. I don't like my job and I would prefer to live in a big city. I'm from France but I am fluent in Spanish and I speak reasonably good English.

e Hello there, my name's David Delgado. I'm from Australia but my parents are originally from Spain. I've got a degree in computing and I've worked in a number of companies providing IT support and training. My present job is as an IT support manager in a further education college in London. I'm 31 years old. I am bilingual in English and Spanish and I would like to work in a Spanish-speaking country.

Language focus

 ### 4.5 *Qualifications and skills*

Here are some different ways to talk about your qualifications and skills.

I've got a diploma in Business Studies with IT.
I have a degree in marketing.
I have 'A' levels in economics, maths and German.
I've got a diploma in IT for business.
I have fluent French and I can speak German quite well too.
I have a driving licence.
I know how to use a number of software accounts packages.
I am pretty good with computers.
I'm good at working in teams and getting on with colleagues.
I know how to operate switchboards and fax machines.
I studied marketing at university.

Note that in British English it is common to use *have got* instead of *have. Have got* sounds less formal. In the USA it is less common to use *have got.* Be careful, we only use *have got* in the present simple tense. For all other tenses, use *have.*

 'A' levels are the examinations that students in England, Wales and Northern Ireland take when they leave school at the age of 18, usually in 3 or 4 subjects. In Scotland many students finish school a year earlier and take 'Highers' in 5 or 6 subjects. At the age of 16, most children in the UK take exams called GCSEs (General Certificate in Secondary Education) in a larger number of subjects (6-10 usually).

Practice

Write about your qualifications and skills.

I've got ....
I also have ....
I know how to ....
I can ....

I'm good at ....
I'm pretty good with ....
I ....
I also ....

Practise talking about your qualifications and skills. Record yourself. You can read the things you wrote at first, but after a little practice you can record yourself talking without any notes.

4.6 *Talking about your experience*

Who said these things? Try to remember, then look back at **4.4** to check.

1 I have been working for a software company for three years. ____
2 I worked in a bank for two years. ____
3 I've got two years' experience of managing an IT support team. ____
4 I worked in the USA for a number of years. ____
5 I've worked in a number of different companies in Spain and in London. ____
6 For the past 18 months I have been working for a travel company. ____

Simple past or present perfect?

When do you use simple past tense (*I worked ...*) and when do you use present perfect tense (*I have worked ...* or *I have been working ...*)?

a Is Patrick still working for a bank in Dublin now? Yes/No? Tense? ____
b Is Teresa Soliz still working for a real estate company now? Yes/No? Tense? ____

To learn more about these tenses, see **Language Reference** section at the end of the book.

Write about your own work and study experience. Concentrate on getting the tenses right.

I have been working in.................... for ....months/years.
Before that I worked in .... for ....
From 199_ to 199_ I studied ....
I have been studying .... since ....
I studied .... in .... for .... years.

Practise talking about your work and study experience. Record yourself. You can read the things you wrote at first, but after a little practice you can record yourself talking without any notes.

4.7 Pronunciation of past tense endings

Regular verbs form their past tense by adding *-ed* (or just *-d* if the base form of the verb already ends in *-e*).

work → worked	live → lived
visit → visited	telephone → telephoned
call → called	decide → decided

Verbs ending in a consonant followed by *-y* usually form the past tense with *-ied* replacing the *-y* of the base form. But verbs ending in a vowel (*a, e, i, o, u*) followed by *-y* just add *-ed*

study → studied	enjoy → enjoyed
dry → dried	play → played

🎧 **Pronunciation note**

As far as the **sound** or **pronunciation** of the past tense is concerned there are three different endings.

/t/ as in *worked*
/d/ as in *lived, telephoned, called*
/id/ as in *decided, visited, started, ended* (where *-ed* follows *t* or *d*)

The difference between /t/ and /d/ is not important but where the ending is /id/ you should be careful to pronounce the extra syllable.

Which of these end in /id/? Practise saying these sentences. Record yourself and listen to the speaker on the recording.

I decided to come to Spain six months ago.
I worked in the USA before I came here.
I started looking for another job last month.
I finished a temporary job yesterday.
My contract with the company ended in February.

🎧 *Listening 2*

4.8 *Conversation in a bar*

It's six o'clock. Roberto has just finished work. He feels like a drink before he takes the bus home. He meets a friend, Patrick, in the bar.

Listen to their conversation and try to answer these questions. If you haven't got a recording to work with, read the conversation instead.

1 How is Patrick feeling? How do you know?
2 What happened to Patrick?
   a He lost his job?
   b His team lost an important game?
   c His job application was unsuccessful?
3 Which job is he going to apply for now?

Roberto	What's the matter, Patrick? You look down in the dumps.
Patrick	Oh, hi, Roberto. I'm okay. I didn't get that job I told you about. If I don't find something soon, I'll have to head back to Dublin.
Roberto	Let me buy you a drink. What'll it be?
Patrick	Oh thanks. A beer, please.
Roberto	Two beers please.
Roberto	Here you are.
Patrick	Thanks.
Roberto	Did you look in *El Mundo* today. I saw a couple of interesting jobs. Here, look.
Patrick	Accounts clerk. Certificate in book-keeping level 3. No, you know what it's like here, you have to have the right qualifications for this type of thing. I haven't got a certificate in book-keeping.
Roberto	Well, you could give it a go.
Patrick	No, I hate working with figures all day anyway.
Roberto	Wait a minute – what about this one? Bilingual executive assistant needed. Must have fluent Spanish and English, good computing skills, efficient and well organized. US $2,500 a month.
Patrick	Hmm, that sounds okay. A bit vague, though. Probably looking for an attractive blonde secretary.

Roberto Well, you never know. It's worth a try.

Patrick I suppose so. Let me copy down the details. Got a pen I can borrow?

Roberto Oh, don't bother, just keep the paper. I've read it all anyway.

Patrick Thanks, Roberto. By the way, did you watch the match last night?

Roberto Yeah, what a disaster! It makes you wonder how they got this far. I can't see much chance of...

🎧 4.9 *Listen for the details*

Listen to the conversation in **4.8** again.

True or false? Write *T* or *F* next to the statements below to show if they are True or False.

1 Patrick has found a new job in Dublin. **F**

2 He doesn't have a book-keeping qualification.

3 He likes working with numbers and calculations.

4 He is optimistic about one of the jobs.

5 Roberto is trying to encourage Patrick.

6 He lent Patrick a pen.

7 The job of executive assistant is only for a woman.

🎧 4.10 *Keeping a conversation going*

What would you say? Choose an appropriate response to these questions and suggestions. Listen to the recording to check your answers.

Example: 1 c

1 Do you fancy going for a drink after work?	**a**	I know I should. But there's never a good time.
2 Have you got a pen I can borrow?	**b**	No, I didn't. Was it any good?
3 What'll it be?	**c**	No, not tonight. I have a lot of work to finish off.
4 Why don't you apply for it?	**d**	A glass of dry white wine for me, please.
5 You really should take a holiday.	**e**	I suppose I could give it a try.
6 By the way, did you watch the football last night?	**f**	Sure. Here you are.

Reading 2

4.11 *Layout of a business letter*

C/ Prim 19
4th floor
28004 Madrid

Telephone 91 523 97 80
E-mail pat.kiely@yahoo.es

The Personnel Manager
International Insurance SA
C/ Villanueva 29
28001 Madrid

20th April

Dear Sir or Madam

I would like to apply for the position of bilingual executive
assistant, which I saw in today's edition of *El Mundo*.

As you will see from my CV, I have a diploma in Business and IT
and experience of administration in the Bank of Ireland. English is
my first language but I have very good spoken and written
Spanish and I can also speak French. I have good IT skills and am
familiar with a number of IT applications.

I am available for interview at any time and, if my application is
successful, I will be able to start work almost immediately.

Yours faithfully

P. Kiely

Patrick O. Kiely

Look at Patrick's letter below and answer these questions.

1 Where does Patrick write his address?
2 Where does he put his name?
3 Where do you put the name and address of the person you are writing to?
4 What do you write at the beginning and end of the letter if you don't know the person's name?

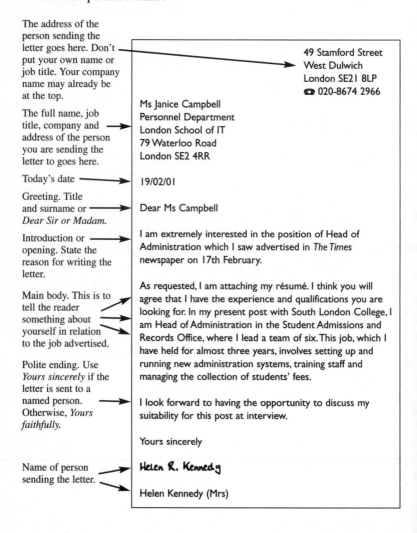

The address of the person sending the letter goes here. Don't put your own name or job title. Your company name may already be at the top.

49 Stamford Street
West Dulwich
London SE21 8LP
☎ 020-8674 2966

The full name, job title, company and address of the person you are sending the letter to goes here.

Ms Janice Campbell
Personnel Department
London School of IT
79 Waterloo Road
London SE2 4RR

Today's date

19/02/01

Greeting. Title and surname or *Dear Sir or Madam.*

Dear Ms Campbell

Introduction or opening. State the reason for writing the letter.

I am extremely interested in the position of Head of Administration which I saw advertised in *The Times* newspaper on 17th February.

Main body. This is to tell the reader something about yourself in relation to the job advertised.

As requested, I am attaching my résumé. I think you will agree that I have the experience and qualifications you are looking for. In my present post with South London College, I am Head of Administration in the Student Admissions and Records Office, where I lead a team of six. This job, which I have held for almost three years, involves setting up and running new administration systems, training staff and managing the collection of students' fees.

Polite ending. Use *Yours sincerely* if the letter is sent to a named person. Otherwise, *Yours faithfully.*

I look forward to having the opportunity to discuss my suitability for this post at interview.

Yours sincerely

Name of person sending the letter.

Helen R. Kennedy

Helen Kennedy (Mrs)

Ending the letter

In **British English** you end the letter with *Yours faithfully* if you don't know the name of the person you are writing to. If you know the name, it is important to put it at the top of the letter, and then end the letter with *Yours sincerely*.

It is much better to find out the name of the person who will receive your letter and then put that at the top of the letter.

David Grantly
Personnel Manager
International Insurance SA
Etc.
Dear Mr Grantly
...
...
Yours sincerely

In **American English** the convention is slightly different. You can use the following options:

Personal, less formal	*Sincerely yours/Yours Sincerely/Sincerely/ Cordially yours*
Fairly formal	*Yours truly/Very truly yours/Yours very truly*
Very formal	*Respectfully yours/Yours (very) respectfully*

Unit 5 gives more practice in writing application letters, CVs and résumés.

🎧 *Listening 3*

4.12 *In the office*

Pierre and Silvia work for International Insurance SA in Madrid, Spain. It is the end of the day but Pierre is still working. Listen to the conversation and identify some problems facing Pierre.

Silvia	Hello, Pierre. I'm just on my way out. How about a quick drink?
Pierre	Oh hi Silvia. No thanks. I've still got a lot to do. I'm leaving for London on Tuesday and I haven't even sorted out all the arrangements, let alone prepared all the papers for the meeting.
Silvia	Anything I can do?
Pierre	No, thanks, it's all right. I'll manage. I'm leaving in about half an hour anyway.
Silvia	You work too hard. You really should have an assistant.
Pierre	I know, I know. There's no point in me staying much longer, anyway, I can't send these e-mails out. The system is giving me trouble again.
Silvia	It works okay for me, Pierre. You just need to take the time to learn how to use it properly. Or get yourself a new assistant. Why don't you ask personnel to advertise for someone?
Pierre	As a matter of fact I did. The advert came out in the newspaper today. I just hope that the person they find stays a bit longer than the last two people I had. The last woman they sent me only stayed a couple of weeks.
Silvia	They will, Pierre, if you are a bit nicer to them. Just because you work 12 hours a day, it doesn't mean everyone else wants to.
Pierre	All right, I know.

🎧 4.13 *Listen for the details*

Listen to the conversation in **4.11** again.

True or false? Write *T* or *F* next to the statements below to show if they are True or False.

1 Pierre is going to have a drink with Silvia. **f**
2 Pierre is not ready for his trip to London next week. ___
3 Pierre's secretary is still working too. ___
4 Pierre doesn't know how to use the e-mail system very well. ___
5 The personnel department is trying to find Pierre a new assistant. ___
6 Pierre's last assistant was a woman. ___
7 Pierre's last assistant worked for him for a long time. ___
8 Silvia thinks Pierre is not nice to his assistants. ___

Rewrite the false sentences in your notebook to make them true:

Example: *Pierre isn't going to have a drink with Silvia. He's too busy.*

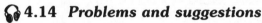 4.14 *Problems and suggestions*

A Match the problems with a suggestion from the list below. Listen to the recording to check your answers.

Example: 1 e

Problems

1 I can't get this printer to work.
2 I'm having problems with these figures.
3 There's something wrong with the photocopier.
4 The lift isn't working, I'm afraid.
5 My car has broken down. Something to do with the steering lock.

Suggestions

a Why don't we take the lift at the other entrance?
b Have you tried switching it off and on again?
c You should take out breakdown cover.
d Why don't you let me have a look at them?
e Have you called the helpdesk?

B What suggestions would you give these people?

Mike:	I don't have time to make all my own travel arrangements.
Alicia:	I'm fed up with this job.
Alexandra:	My boss expects me to work 12 hours a day!
Paul:	I can't open my e-mails.
Julie:	I never have any money left at the end of the month.

C Write some more problems and suggestions.

Practise with a friend. One of you describes a problem. The other one makes an appropriate suggestion.

Lesson summary

Here are some of the things you practised in this lesson:

● Understanding job advertisements.

● Talking about your qualifications:
> *I've got a diploma in Accountancy.*
> *I have a degree in Business Studies from London University.*

● Talking about work experience:
> *I worked for the Bank of Ireland for three years.*
> *I've been working here since 1999.*

● Problems and suggestions:
> *I'm having trouble with this computer.*
> *Why don't you call the technician?*

Suggestions for further practice

1 Write some more profiles of qualifications and experience, like the ones in **4.4**. You can think of people you know and write profiles for them.

2 Look for job advertisements in a newspaper (for example the *International Herald Tribune*, the *Financial Times*) or a website that advertises jobs. See how well you can understand them. If you find any words or abbreviations you do not know, first try to guess the meanings, then look in your business English dictionary to check if you were right. Use your vocabulary notebook to record any useful words or expressions.

3 Write a dialogue about a company problem and suggestions for solving it.

4 Find some business letters in different languages and compare the conventions for organizing information.

5 | LETTERS AND CVs

In this unit you will practise:
◆ understanding job requirements
◆ analysing a job advertisement
◆ writing an effective job application letter
◆ writing a CV or résumé

Language:
◆ professional qualities and characteristics
◆ positive action verbs to describe achievements
◆ useful phrases for opening and closing a job application letter
◆ key skills and abilities

Introduction

5.1 *Applying for a job*

There are two kinds of job application. You may be applying for a job that is advertised, in which case you should have quite a lot of information about what the employer is looking for. Or you may be writing to companies to ask for a job, even though no job has been advertised.

In both cases, you need to make yourself seem attractive to the company as a potential employee, so that they will invite you to an interview. The main purpose of your application is to get an interview. So, you need to "sell yourself". The activity below will help you to do this.

A What kind of person are you? How would you describe yourself? Tick the adjectives and phrases you think apply to yourself? Add any others you think describe you well.

kind	ambitious	easy-going
hard-working	a good communicator	articulate
generous	a team player	helpful
smart (appearance)	determined	intelligent
well organized	careful	laid back
punctual	ruthless	sympathetic
enthusiastic	motivated	independent
good at managing people		

NB Notice that *smart* in British English refers to your appearance and your clothes. In the US it is often used to mean intelligent or clever.

B Which of your qualities do you think an employer might like? Which qualities are relevant to all jobs? Which ones only apply to certain kinds of jobs, e.g. a salesman, a manager, a secretary?

Reading 1

5.2 *A job advertisement*

If you are writing a letter in response to an advertisement, it is very important to match yourself to the selection criteria in the advertisement or job description. Look at the advertisement on the next page for clues about what this company is looking for.

Look at the sentences below and on page 56. Which ones would you include in a letter applying for this job? Tick (✔) the ones that you think are appropriate and put a cross (✗) next to those that are not appropriate.

a I have a full driving licence and I would be happy to travel.

b I am married with two young children.

c I have experience of providing IT support for a range of businesses including travel and retail.

d I am in good health and I enjoy sports activities.

e When I was a student I also did voluntary work caring for children in a hospital.

f Although my main degree is in distributed computing systems, I also completed courses in graphic design and usability design.

more than one job

knowledge about this established company

computing knowledge

knowledge of world of business

design

qualification

experience

able to work with business clients

initiate change

solve problems

complete projects

mobile, driving licence

good communicator

teamwork

ambitious

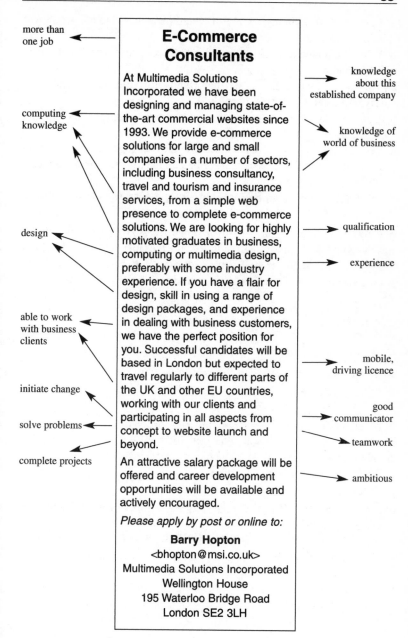

E-Commerce Consultants

At Multimedia Solutions Incorporated we have been designing and managing state-of-the-art commercial websites since 1993. We provide e-commerce solutions for large and small companies in a number of sectors, including business consultancy, travel and tourism and insurance services, from a simple web presence to complete e-commerce solutions. We are looking for highly motivated graduates in business, computing or multimedia design, preferably with some industry experience. If you have a flair for design, skill in using a range of design packages, and experience in dealing with business customers, we have the perfect position for you. Successful candidates will be based in London but expected to travel regularly to different parts of the UK and other EU countries, working with our clients and participating in all aspects from concept to website launch and beyond.

An attractive salary package will be offered and career development opportunities will be available and actively encouraged.

Please apply by post or online to:

Barry Hopton
<bhopton@msi.co.uk>
Multimedia Solutions Incorporated
Wellington House
195 Waterloo Bridge Road
London SE2 3LH

g I prefer to work on my own but I would be prepared to cooperate with others and work in a team.

h While I am able to work independently, successful teamwork has been a key part of my present job.

i This post interests me as an opportunity to build on my skills and develop a career in my chosen field.

j I am interested in improving my salary and conditions and this job seems to offer me this opportunity.

k My communication and teamwork skills, together with strong commitment and enthusiasm, have helped me to complete a number of challenging projects.

l My father ran his own business, and many of my friends and relatives are in the business field.

See **Key to Exercises** on p. 194 for suggested answers. It is essential to match your skills and qualifications to the job that is advertised. Sometimes an employer will send a detailed job description and or a person specification. You should try to address all the points asked for.

Reading 2

5.3 *An application letter*

Read the letter and answer the following questions.

1 Where does Chris Andrews live?

2 What is his present job?

3 What qualifications does he hold?

4 What is the title of the job he is applying for?

5 What date was the job advertised in the *Daily News*?

6 What is Barry Hopton's position?

7 Who does he work for?

8 Do you think Chris looks like a suitable applicant for this job? Why?/Why not?

9 Do you think he has written an effective job application letter? How could it be improved?

9 Greenfields Avenue
South Ealing
London W5 5RN

Mr Barry Hopton
Personnel Manager
Multimedia Solutions Incorporated
Wellington House
195 Waterloo Bridge Road
London SE2 3LH

17th May

Dear Mr Hopton

I would like to apply for one of the posts of e-commerce consultant with your company which I saw advertised in today's *Daily News*. This post is exactly what I am looking for, and at the same time I am confident that I have the skills and experience your company needs.

My first degree, in IT with Business Studies, has given me a good understanding of how these two fields are related, as well as the practical IT skills to advise business clients on their needs and implement solutions. In the two years since I graduated I have put these skills to practical use as Web Designer with West London College of Higher Education. In addition I have completed freelance projects for small businesses and taken courses in graphic design and usability design. The post you advertised interests me greatly as an opportunity to build on my skills and develop a career in my chosen field. I'm also attracted by the variety of work that your company would offer and I would enjoy the opportunity to work in other parts of the UK and Europe.

My CV is attached and further information about myself, and links to Internet projects I have worked on can be found at my website: http://www.aol.com/homepages/andrewscj/index.htm. I am available for interview at any time and I would like the opportunity to demonstrate that I have the necessary qualities.

Yours sincerely

C. Andrews

Chris Andrews

5.4 *Tips for writing an application letter*

Look at this list of "Do's and Don'ts" for writing application letters. Choose some of the tips and decide if they are do's or don'ts. Tick (✔) the do's and put a cross (✘) next to the don'ts.

Do's and Don'ts

1 Apply for a job that the company doesn't have.
2 Be clear and concise.
3 Be positive – use positive words like *"achieved"* and *"success"*.
4 Focus on what you have to offer an employer.
5 Have your cover letter checked by at least one other person before you post it.
6 Know what job you are applying for.
7 Make your enthusiasm for the job and the company very clear.
8 Be dishonest. Make sure you are able to discuss or explain any sentence in your application. Any information you give may be used in the interview.
9 Match yourself to the selection criteria listed in the advertisement/ position description.
10 Sound desperate.
11 Use a word processor and laser printer to produce your letter.
12 Use negative language, e.g. talking about the bad things in your present job.
13 Use simple and uncomplicated sentences.
14 Clutter up the page with too much information.
15 Use your cover letter as an example of the fact that you can write a professional looking business letter.
16 Give examples of things you have done, to show that you have the skills you say you have.

Check your answers in the **Key** at the back of the book.

Can you think of any more tips? Write them in your notebook. For example:

● Don't send a handwritten letter, unless you are specifically asked to.
● Do try to find out the name of the person your application should be addressed to.

5.5 *Analysing an advertisement*

Look at this job advertisement and analyse it in the same way as the advertisement in **5.1**. Or, if you prefer, find an advertisement for a job you are interested in, and use that instead.

The questions below might help you. Underline or draw an arrow to the relevant information in the advertisement.

1 Does the job require IT skills?

2 What qualifications are required?

3 How much experience is required?

4 What kind of products or services are involved?

5 Are there opportunities for promotion?

6 Will the job require travel?

7 Do you think communication skills are important?

8 Do you think foreign language skills are required?

9 Is the job only for British people?

10 What information is provided about the company?

11 How many jobs are available?

12 Will training be provided?

Business Graduates

We are a large financial consultancy agency looking to recruit between 50 and 100 executive trainees for posts throughout our European network. After initial training, successful applicants will be based in one of our regional offices, providing financial consultancy and planning advice on products including pensions, life assurance, savings, investments and taxes.

Good package plus incentives and long term prospects. Interested?

Phone 01723 590 8080 or e-mail personnel@fse.com

FINANCIAL SERVICES EUROPE

Make some notes on some things about yourself that you would highlight in your application letter or CV.

Language focus

5.6 *More tips and useful language*

Here are some ideas about how to describe yourself effectively in job application letters and CVs.

1 Think carefully about the purpose of writing an application letter. This can include the following things:

- To inform the employer that you are interested in the job;
- To persuade the employer that you are a suitable candidate;
- To make sure that they look at your CV and invite you for an interview;
- To suggest areas that will be discussed in the interview;
- To show that you can communicate clearly and effectively in writing;
- To show that you know how to write a business letter and present it in a professional, attractive way;
- To make you look professional;
- To give the reader some idea about your personality.

2 **The opening** should state which job you are applying for, possibly say where you found out about it, and show that you are positive and enthusiastic about the job. Here are some possible phrases that you could include:

You advertisement for the post of executive assistant in today's Times interests me greatly because ...

I am confident that I have the skills and experience you are looking for.

I have the commitment and expertise that I believe are necessary to succeed in this job.

From your advertisement it seems that you need a person who can ...

I believe I am exactly the kind of person you are looking for.

I can offer the professional skills and motivation needed to ...

Given the opportunity I am sure that I could successfully fulfil your requirements.

3 In **the main body of your letter** you should match the job requirements to the skills and refer the reader to relevant parts of your CV or résumé. It is enough to write about two or three key skills you have. Write a short paragraph about each of these. It is important to provide examples of specific skills and achievements relevant to the job.

As you will see from my CV, I graduated from ...

In my previous job, I successfully trained the customer care team to ....

I was responsible for introducing a new system for recording contacts which contributed to a 25 per cent increase in sales.

Use positive action verbs that highlight your achievements:

I started	*I introduced*	*I developed*	*I completed*
I trained	*I achieved*	*I increased*	*I organized*
I led	*I managed*	*I improved*	*I accomplished*
I trained	*I planned*	*I prepared*	*I was responsible for*

4 Closing the letter

I would be happy to discuss my suitability for this position further.

I look forward to meeting you in person to discuss what I can offer your company.

An interview would give me the opportunity to show you the commitment I could offer in this job.

I look forward to meeting you and finding out more about the challenges this job could offer me.

I am confident that an interview will confirm my suitability for this post.

I will be happy to supply references and any further information you require.

Thank you, in anticipation, for considering my application.

I am sure that the attached CV will convince you that I have the necessary skills for this position.

5.7 *Your own letter of application*

1 Write your own job application letter for one of the job advertisements in **Unit 4** or **5**. Or find a suitable advertisement in a newspaper or on the Internet to apply for.

2 Books on business letters, books on applying for jobs, and several Internet sites include sample job application letters. Find one or more of these and compare them with your letter. Some suggestions for further reading and links are provided at the end of this Unit.

Patrick David Kiely

Contact Details

Calle Prim 19
4th floor
28004 Madrid

Telephone 91 523 97 80
E-mail <pat.kiely@yahoo.es>

Education

1995–1998   Dorset College of Further Education, Dublin. Advanced Diploma
            in IT and Business Administration.
1989–1995   St Joseph's College, Dublin. (Leaving Certificates including
            grade A in Spanish, Maths and Economics, grade B in Physics,
            English and Art.)

Employment History

1999–2001   Bank of Ireland, Dublin. Banking officer. All aspects of local
            branch banking. Counter cashier, responsible for receiving and
            issuing money, foreign exchange, accurately debiting and
            crediting accounts; advising customers on loans and financial
            products; sorting out problems and customer care.
1996–1998   (Part time) Salesperson in National Gallery of Ireland,
            Publications Department. Sales and packaging of art books,
            prints and cards. Stocktaking and record keeping.
1998–1999   (Summer vacation job) Comlink computers. Advising private
            customers and small businesses on their IT requirements. Sales,
            delivery and installation of PCs. Answering technical queries and
            dealing with IT problems.

Other Professional Courses

June 2000   Bank of Ireland. One-week course in foreign exchange.
1996–1997   Dublin Community College (part time evening course). Business
            French.
May 2001   USA College of English & Business, Madrid. HTML & web
            design. Introductory course on web page design and maintenance.

Other skills

            Good IT skills. Proficient user of Word, Excel, Access. Internet
            and E-mail packages. Basic knowledge of HTML and Microsoft
            FrontPage (web page design).
            Fluent Spanish (written and spoken).
            French (fairly fluent spoken, good written).
            English (mother tongue).

5.8 *CVs and résumés*

A Here are some questions about Patrick. Find the answers in the CV on p. 62. NB if the information is not available in the CV, just write *No information*.

1 Where does Patrick live?
2 How many years did he study at Dorset College?
3 What was the name of his secondary school?
4 What is his date of birth?
5 Is he married?
6 Does he have any children?
7 Does he have an e-mail address?
8 What is his postal address?
9 Where did he work part time while he was a student?
10 What subjects was he good at in his secondary school?
11 Which language does he speak better, French or Spanish?
12 What were his duties at Comlink Computers?
13 Which job does Patrick put first on his CV, the earliest or the latest?

B How could this CV be improved? Do you think Patrick should include more information? Is there anything he should leave out? Would you advise him to add extra sections to his CV (for example, about his hobbies and interests)?

C From the information in his CV, does Patrick seem to have the right experience and qualifications for the job of bilingual executive assistant?

5.9 *Your own CV or résumé*

1 Have you already prepared a CV or résumé? Is it up to date? Are you happy with it? Write/rewrite it keeping in mind one of the jobs advertised in **Unit 4** or **5**, or a real job advertisement.

2 Find some sample CVs and compare them with your own. Some suggestions for further reading and links are provided at the end of this unit.

Lesson summary

Here are some of the things you practised in this lesson:

- Adjectives to describe your qualities: *well organized, articulate, punctual, ambitious, motivated* (see **5.1**).

- Looking carefully at job advertisements to see what kind of person they are looking for (see **5.2** and **5.5**).

- Writing effective application letters (see **5.1–5.7**).
  Useful opening phrases:
  > *Your advertisement for the post of executive assistant in today's* Times *interests me greatly because ...*
  > *I believe I am exactly the kind of person you are looking for.*

  Highlighting your key skills:
  > *As you will see from my CV, I graduated from ...*
  > *In my previous job, I was responsible for introducing ...*

  Using positive language and describing your achievements:
  > *I achieved ...; I introduced...; started, trained, improved, was responsible for, planned*

  Useful closing phrases:
  > *I look forward to meeting you in person to discuss what I can offer your company.*
  > *I will be happy to supply references and any further information you require.*
  > *Thank you, in anticipation, for considering my application.*

- CVs and résumés (see **5.8–5.10**).

Suggestions for further practice

1 Look at two different job advertisements for similar jobs that you might apply for. Make lists of the key skills and qualities that are asked for in both advertisements. What things are the same for both advertisements? What things are different?

2 Write your CV and give it to a colleague to look at. Ask your colleague to suggest improvements.

3 Find some sample application letters, either in your company, or on the Internet or in books. Draw a circle around sentences and sections you

think are very good, and underline the parts you don't like so much. Make a note in your notebook of useful sentences and expressions used in the opening, the main body and the closing of the letters. Make a note of the positive verbs used to describe achievements.

4 The following websites have useful information on writing job application letters and CVs.

http://www.ruthvilmi.net/hut/help/writing_instructions/

http://www.swin.edu.au/corporate/careers/coverletter.htm

http://owl.english.purdue.edu/handouts/pw/

http://www1.umn.edu/ohr/ecep/resume/

6 | A JOB INTERVIEW

In this unit you will practise:
- ◆ taking part in a job interview
- ◆ discussing candidates for a job

Language:
- ◆ qualities and characteristics
- ◆ similarities and differences
- ◆ present perfect continuous and past simple tense
- ◆ expressing opinions, agreeing and disagreeing
- ◆ making decisions and giving reasons

Introduction

6.1 *Interview questions*

- How many job interviews have you had? How did you feel? Were any of the questions unexpected or were you well prepared for everything? How did you feel? Nervous? Confident? Relaxed?
- What questions do you expect to get asked in a job interview?
- Have you ever interviewed someone for a job yourself? How did you prepare for the interview? How did you plan the questions?

Interviewers are likely to include some questions based on the candidate's CV and application letter, as well as some general questions that all the candidates will be asked. There may be some areas that the interviewers cannot ask about because of company policy or employment laws. For example, in the UK it is not usual to ask about a candidate's family, number of children, their childcare arrangements, etc.

A Look back at Patrick Kiely's application letter in Unit 4, p. 47 and his CV in Unit 5, p. 62. Imagine you are going to interview him for the job at International Insurance. Write down some questions you would like to ask him.

B Write down answers to the questions you thought of.

Do you think it is important to be completely truthful in a job interview? Or is it okay to lie about things like your interest in the company and the job you are applying for, or your reasons for leaving your previous job?

Listening 1

6.2 *An interview*

Patrick Kiely is having an interview at International Insurance, for the job of bilingual executive assistant. There are three interviewers, David Grantly, the Head of Personnel, and Silvia Becatto and Pierre Croyden, who are senior executives in the company. If Patrick gets the job, he will be working with Pierre.

The interview has already been going on for about 15 minutes and Patrick has already talked about his business studies and his previous job.

Look at David Grantly's interview notes. He has made a note of three questions he wants to ask Patrick. As you listen to the interview, note down Patrick's answers.

1. Left his previous job with the Bank of Ireland 6 months ago. Why?

2. What has he been doing since he arrived in Madrid?

3. Plans for the future? Settle in Madrid or move back to Ireland?

Silvia From what you have told us, Mr Kiely, it seems that you were doing well with the Bank of Ireland. Would you mind telling us why you decided to leave?

Patrick Yes, of course. Really there were a number of reasons. Firstly, I really wanted to travel and work abroad, particularly in Spain. That has always been my ambition. Secondly, my partner, who is from Madrid, was offered a very good job with an American bank here in Madrid. So we decided that this would be a good time to move here. I felt I had been at the Bank of Ireland long enough to gain a lot of useful experience, and there was not much opportunity for me to get an overseas posting with the bank, not in the near future anyway.

David You left that job about six months ago, is that right? What have you been doing in that time?

Patrick Well, as I said in my letter I have been working really hard on my Spanish and doing some other courses as well. Obviously I have been applying for jobs, too. There are not that many opportunities in the banking sector at the moment, although that is not the only area I'm interested in. I've had a number of interviews and I have turned down a couple of offers. This job is one that would match my skills well, though, and I really feel that it is the kind of thing I am looking for.

Pierre How about your long-term plans, do you think you will stay in Spain or do you hope to move back to Ireland, or somewhere else, perhaps?

Patrick Well I wouldn't like to promise that I'll definitely be here for the rest of my life, but I really like Madrid, my partner's family live here, and so at the moment we feel pretty settled in Madrid.

David Right. Well, I don't think we have any more questions for you. Pierre? No, okay, perhaps there are some things you would like to ask us about the job or the company?

Patrick Yes, you mentioned opportunities to travel, and that was one thing that attracted me to this job. Could you tell me some more about that?

6.3 *Listen for the details*

Listen to the conversation in **6.2** again.

True or false? Write *T* or *F* next to the statements below to show if they are True or False.

1 Patrick is interested in travelling.
2 His girlfriend is Irish too.
3 This is his first interview since he arrived in Spain.
4 He has been offered some jobs already.
5 He has been doing some language classes in Madrid.
6 He left the Bank of Ireland because he didn't like his job.

Language focus

 6.4 *The right tense*

Choose the right tense. Try to complete the exercise first, without reading the dialogue or listening to it. Then listen to the recording to check your answers.

1 From what you have told us, Mr Kiely, it seems that you were doing well with the Bank of Ireland. Would you mind telling us why you *decided / have decided* to leave?

2 I *felt / have felt* I had been at the Bank of Ireland long enough to gain a lot of useful experience.

3 You left that job about six months ago, is that right? What *did you do / have you been doing* in that time?

4 Well, as I *said / have said* in my letter I *worked / have worked / have been working* really hard on my Spanish and doing some other courses as well.

5 Obviously I *applied / have been applying* for jobs, too.

6 *I had / I've had* a number of interviews and I *turned down / have turned down* a couple of offers.

In general we use **present perfect continuous** (*have been doing / has been doing*) for recent activities, for the things happening in the period up to the present. These activities might still be continuing, or they might have stopped. We use **past simple** tense for activities in a time period that is finished. So, for example, Patrick left Ireland six months ago. If he talks about the time he was in Ireland, or his previous job, he will probably use the past simple tense.

Practice

A Think about your recent activities. Have you been playing a lot of sport recently? Have you been taking a course or learning something? Have you been working hard? What have you been working on over the last few days and weeks? Write some sentences.

Examples:

> *I've been working extremely hard the last three weeks. I have been preparing a report on a new product my company would like to offer.*
> *I've been playing tennis regularly for the last two years.*

B Think about your last job, your last school, or, if you have finished studying, think back to the time when you were a student. Write about some of your activities then. What was your life/work/studies like then? What kinds of activities were you involved in?

Examples:

> *I played a lot of tennis and football when I was a student.*
> *I shared an apartment in New York with two of my colleagues.*
> *I worked on product development for a year, then I worked in the marketing department.*

For further information, see the **Language Reference** section at the end of the book. Look out for more examples of these tenses in the dialogues and in your reading.

🎧 Listening 2

6.5 Another interview

Now David, Pierre and Silvia are interviewing another candidate, Teresa Soliz.

Listen to the conversation and make notes about Teresa.

Pierre   According to your CV you work for a real estate company. You've been there for quite a long time, haven't you?

Teresa   Yes, that's right, three years.

Pierre   So I was wondering, why do you want to leave now?

Teresa   Well, I do like my job, and the money is good. But anyway three years is the longest I've been in any job and I feel it's time for a change. Besides, I really want to do something a bit different from just secretarial work. I feel this job will offer me that.

Pierre   Oh yes, definitely. The work is very varied and we are looking for someone to take on quite a lot of responsibility working in my department. But there would also be administrative duties, some correspondence, typing reports and handling e-mails. Is that what you expected?

Teresa   That sounds okay.

Silvia   Well, thank you very much, Miss Soliz. Perhaps there are some questions you would like to ask us?

Teresa   Yes, of course, I think you have explained everything about this job, and I am really interested in it. I wanted to find out about longer-term prospects in the company.

Silvia   Of course, well we are looking for someone to work with Pierre and support him in all aspects of his work. It would be a good opportunity to learn about all aspects of insurance, not just loss adjustment which is Pierre's responsibility.

David   This is a large company, and we advertise posts internally wherever possible, so once you have some experience in this post there would certainly be opportunities for promotion.

Teresa   How about training?

David   Yes, of course, we offer quite a few programmes in-company and we also send people on courses outside. We would look at your needs and put together an initial package of courses. But it is also our policy to allow employees to . . .

🎧 6.6 *Listen for the details*

Listen again to the conversation in **6.5**.

True or false? Write *T* or *F* next to the statements below to show if they are True or False.

1 Teresa is working for a real estate company at the moment.
2 Teresa left her job with the real estate company after three years.

3 Pierre's department at International Insurance deals with loss adjustment.
4 The job Teresa has applied for only involves secretarial work.
5 There are opportunities to transfer to another job in International Insurance.

6.7 *Vocabulary*

Try to complete these phrases without listening again or reading the scripts of the interviews (**6.2** and **6.5**). Then look at the scripts to check your answers. If no words are missing, just leave the space blank.

1 Patrick's interview
   a There was not much opportunity _____ me to get an overseas posting _____ the bank.
   b What have you been doing _____ that time?
   c I have been working really hard _____ my Spanish.
   d I have turned _____ a couple of offers.
   e I really feel that it is the kind of thing I am looking _____ .
   f Do you think you will stay in Spain or do you hope to move _____ to Ireland?
   g Perhaps there are some things you would like to ask _____ us about the job.
   h Could you tell me some more _____ that?

2 Teresa's interview
   a I feel it's time _____ a change.
   b You have explained everything _____ this job, and I am really interested _____ it.
   c I really want to do something a bit different _____ just secretarial work.
   d We are looking for someone to take _____ quite a lot of responsibility.
   e We would look _____ your needs and put _____ an initial package.

3 Find the phrases above that mean the same as these words:

   a to refuse, not to accept   **c** to be responsible for
   b not the same as   **d** examine, discuss, think about

Language focus

6.8 *Qualities for the job*

What do you think are the most important things that business employers look for when they are recruiting new staff? Knowledge of business? Knowledge about a particular sector of industry? IT skills? Punctuality and smart appearance?

Obviously it depends on the job. But a recent survey of employers showed that there was a lot of agreement about the most important things they look for when they recruit graduates.

The list below shows the top 17 out of 62 different attributes (or characteristics) employers would like graduate employees to have. Look at the list. Which ones do you think are surprising? Are there any other things you expected to see on the list?

The most important attributes employers expect from graduates

1 Willingness to learn	2 Commitment	3 Dependability
4 Self-motivation	5 Teamwork	6 Communication skills
7 Co-operation	8 Drive & energy	9 Self management
10 Motivation to achieve	11 Problem-solving ability	12 Analytical ability
13 Flexibility	14 Initiative	15 Logical argument
16 Adaptability	17 Numeracy	

[*Source: Managing Higher Education*, Issue 2, 1996]

Practice

A Rate yourself in relation to these characteristics. Give yourself a score out of 10.

B Write sentences about yourself using the adjectives that correspond to the attribute. You can use the following modifiers:

High amount of the characteristic: *very, highly, extremely, really*
Medium amount of the characteristic: *fairly, reasonably, quite, pretty*
Low amount of the characteristic: *not very*

Examples:

> *I'm **very** willing to learn.*
> *I'm **extremely** committed.*
> *I have got **quite a lot of** drive.*
> *I'm **fairly** good at working in teams.*
> *I'm **not very** good at oral communication skills. / I'm **not a very** good communicator.*
> *I'm **pretty** good with figures (numerate).*
> *I think I'm a **fairly** flexible person.*
> *I'm **highly** motivated.*

 Listening 3

6.9 Making a choice

After the interviews, David, Silvia and Pierre discussed the candidates. Listen to their discussion and answer these questions:

1 How many candidates did they interview for this job?
2 Which one did they choose?
3 Who was their second choice?
4 Which candidate did they feel was more relaxed? More ambitious? Had better Spanish? Better English? Was better qualified?

David	Well, what do you think?
Silvia	My feeling is that it is a choice between the last girl and the Irish chap. They both seemed very competent and enthusiastic.
David	I agree, they were clearly the best of the five we interviewed. What about you, Pierre? After all, whoever gets the job will be working closely with you.
Pierre	It's a difficult choice. Miss, er, Soliz, has a lot of experience, and she is clearly ambitious. She seems to have all the qualifications we are looking for. But so does Mr Kiely.
David	He hasn't worked for six months, since he came to Madrid.
Pierre	I know. But it can't be easy for someone coming here from abroad.

Silvia	And he hasn't wasted his time. He has taken some IT courses and he has been studying Spanish.
Pierre	I think we should take him. I have a feeling he would be more likely to stay with the company. He made it very clear how keen he was to get the job.
David	Do you think his Spanish is up to it?
Pierre	His Spanish seemed pretty good. I suppose he would need someone to check any important letters he wrote. And his English is obviously not a problem.
Silvia	Yes, I felt that his Spanish was as good as her English. And he seemed to be very confident and relaxed. That should make it easier for him to get on with you, Pierre.
Pierre	Are you suggesting I'm difficult to work with?
Silvia	Only joking, Pierre. Seriously, what do you think?
Pierre	I agree with you. Also, he did say he could start immediately. We are desperate for the help in my department. David?
David	That's fine with me. I'll offer him the job, to start as soon as possible. Miss Soliz is our second choice. If you agree, I'll let her know that if a similar job comes up, we would be happy to offer it to her.
Pierre	Fine. Thanks a lot David, Silvia.
David	You are welcome. I'll talk to you after I have spoken to Mr Kiely.

6.10 *Useful expressions*

Find these expressions in the conversation in **6.9**. Then try to match them with their synonyms.

1 to get on with someone _____

2 to let someone know _____

3 to be up to it _____

4 to come up _____

a to inform someone

b to be able to do something, to be good enough

c to happen unexpectedly

d to have a good relationship with someone, able to work together

Look for any other words or expressions in the conversations.

Language focus

 6.11 *Comparisons*

Look at these different ways of comparing people.

> Same:
>> *Both candidates were **equally** enthusiastic/well qualified/good at expressing themselves.*
>> *Teresa and Patrick **both** have very good IT skills.*
>> *I felt Teresa was **just as** ambitious **as** Patrick.*
>
> Different:
>> *Patrick seemed **more confident than** Teresa.*
>> *Teresa seemed **less confident than** Patrick.*
>> *I felt Teresa was **not as confident as** Patrick.*
>> *Patrick **had more confidence than** Teresa.*
>> *Patrick could start **sooner**.*
>> *Teresa was **better qualified** for the position.*
>
> Small differences:
>> *Patrick could start **a little/a bit/slightly** sooner than Teresa.*
>> *Teresa was **not quite** as enthusiastic as Patrick.*
>> *Patrick's Spanish is **almost** as good as Teresa's English.*
>
> Big differences:
>> *I thought Teresa was **much** more experienced.*
>> *She didn't seem **nearly** as enthusiastic as Patrick.*
>> *In my opinion she was **nowhere near as** enthusiastic about the job.*

Practice

A Look at the interview notes about two candidates for a secretarial job with International Insurance services. Write sentences comparing the two candidates.

B Write a dialogue of the discussion about these candidates, based on these notes. You can use the conversation in **6.9** as a model.

Marisol Delgado	Virginia Ferrufino
Very fast typing speed! Made a few mistakes though	Fast typing
7 years' experience	Very accurate typist - only made one mistake
Very good English, also a little Italian	4½ years' experience
Could start in 2 weeks	Speaks excellent English, good French, some German
Present job - she earns around $1,700 a month	Could start immediately
Very ambitious. Would she stay in this job long??	Earns $2,000 in present job. Can we match that?
No problem with 8.30 a.m. start time	Cannot start work before 9.30 a.m.
Seemed a little nervous. Perhaps not a very confident person	Seems very relaxed and confident
Excellent knowledge of computers. Good with PowerPoint, Excel, knows about databases	Seems very knowledgeable about Word but not much experience with PowerPoint and other applications

Lesson summary

Here are some of the things you practised in this lesson:

● Talking about recent activities:

I've been working on a number of projects for my company.
I've been playing football quite a lot recently.
I've been working in the marketing department since last May.

- Talking about activities in the past:

    In my previous job I worked on a number of similar projects.

    I took courses on e-commerce and web page design as part of my degree.

    I worked in teams a lot when I was with the Bank of Ireland.

- Talking about your attributes, using modifiers:

    *I think I'm **pretty good** at working in teams.*

    *She is **extremely** good at solving problems.*

    *He's **not very** confident but he seems highly motivated.*

    *According to her previous employer, she is **not very** dependable.*

- Comparisons, similarities and differences:

    *Teresa has **more** experience than Patrick.*

    *He is not **as well** qualified for the job **as** she is.*

    *She is **much more** enthusiastic about the job.*

    *He is **not quite as** confident **as** her.*

Suggestions for further practice

1 Find a book or a website which has advice for successful interviews. Make a list of "do's" and "don'ts" for job interviews. Choose some questions and write answers (for yourself).

2 Practise job interviews with one or two friends. Take it in turns to be the interviewer(s) and the candidate(s).

3 Write a dialogue of part of a job interview, in your company, perhaps for your own job.

4 Think about two people, perhaps two colleagues that you know well. Write some sentences comparing them. Focus on their similarities and differences.

5 Imagine you have interviewed two people for a job or a promotion within your company. Write a dialogue of the discussion between yourself and another interviewer in which you discuss which candidate is most suitable.

6 Make a list of some of the useful expressions in this unit, especially the expressions which combine verbs and prepositions (e.g. *get on with someone, take on, give up*). Practise using them in sentences.

7 CHECK YOUR PROGRESS

7.1 *Vocabulary*

Fill in the missing letters. Can you add any more words?

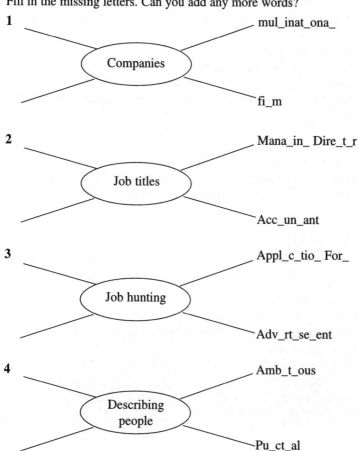

1 Companies
- mul_inat_ona_
- fi_m

2 Job titles
- Mana_in_ Dire_t_r
- Acc_un_ant

3 Job hunting
- Appl_c_tio_ For_
- Adv_rt_se_ent

4 Describing people
- Amb_t_ous
- Pu_ct_al

7.2

Complete these sentences with appropriate words which appeared in **Units 1–6**.

1 Comet is a _____ of Kingfisher plc.
2 Ryanair was _____ in 1985.
3 Paul is in charge of the IT section and he _____ the IT support staff.
4 The Customer Relations Manager _____ _____ complaints from customers.
5 I'd _____ you to meet my colleague David Brown.
6 Both Unilever and Margarine Unie were _____ in marketing household goods.
7 Unilever markets famous brands _____ Dove, Lipton and Magnum ice cream.
8 The two companies _____ in 1930.
9 I know ____ to operate fax machines.
10 For further _____ and an application form, contact ...
11 I have been working in a software company ____ the past three years.
12 My father _____ his own business until he retired last year.
13 I look _____ to meeting you in person.
14 As you will see from my _____ I have a degree in Business Studies.
15 How many candidates _____ they interview for this job?
16 International Insurance _____ Patrick a job and he accepted it.
17 Patrick _____ more confident than Teresa.

🎧 7.3

A reporter would like to interview you for a radio programme about work. Listen to the recording or read and answer these reporter's questions. (If you are not working at the moment, imagine you already have a job.)

1 Who do you work for?
2 What kind of company is that?
3 How long have you been working there?
4 What is your job title?
5 What did you do before you started your current job?
6 How many hours a week do you work?
7 What do you like/dislike about your job?
8 What's the most important quality you need to do this job?

When you have finished, listen to the second part of the recording which contains the complete interview with the questions and suggested answers.

7.4 *Jumbled Sentences*

Fit the two parts of each sentence together, e.g. 1 and f.

1 Microsoft designs and ...
2 I'd like you to meet ...
3 Unilever NV and Unilever plc are the parent companies of what is ...
4 I don't have time to make ...
5 Why don't you ask ...
6 I have a lot of experience ...
7 Paulo was not as ...

a your colleagues to help?
b of working in teams.
c well qualified as Maria-Teresa.
d Patrick Corbet from British Airways.
e all my own travel arrangements.
f manufactures computer software.
g today one of the largest consumer goods businesses in the world.

8 | FINANCE

In this unit you will practise:
◆ talking about figures
◆ listening to a radio broadcast for specific information
◆ making comparisons

Language:
◆ currencies and money
◆ numbers and prices
◆ comparative adjectives
◆ approximate times and figures

Introduction

8.1 *Money and finance questions*

● The *Financial Times* and the *Wall Street Journal* are famous business newspapers in Britain and the United States. What is the most famous business newspaper in your country?

● Bill Gates, the founder of Microsoft, is one of the richest people in the world. How much money do you think he has? $100 million? $500 million? $1,000,000 million? $5,000,000 million?

● Which of the following are connected with stock markets?
The Nikkei, American Express, the FTSE100, Wall Street?

● In Britain the largest note is worth fifty pounds. What's the largest note in your country?

● How much is one US dollar worth in your currency?

Here are three news items. What are they about?
Stock markets? Currency rates? Inflation? Unemployment? Interest rates?

> 1 The most spectacular decline at the start of the year was British Airways, whose share price fell from 420p to 260p in the first quarter of 2000.
>
> 2 The government's aim to bring the number of jobless to below 3.5 million before the next election is not impossible, though it is an ambitious target.
>
> 3 The Bank of Japan has reduced its rate to zero to revive its economy, which has suffered a long-term recession since the early 1990s.

Language focus

8.2 *Discussing figures*

Currencies

In written English, currency symbols are placed before the number but when speaking we usually say the symbol after the number, for example:

$8,000	eight thousand dollars	SR25	twenty-five riyals
€120	one hundred and twenty euros	Y969,000	nine hundred and sixty-nine thousand yen

Note:

£5.94	five pounds ninety-four
$10.87	ten dollars eighty-seven

Decimals

In Britain and the USA we use a point (.) for decimals not a comma (,):

12.56	twelve point five six
2.1 m	two point one million

(However, be careful, as in most other countries it is common to use a comma for decimals e.g. 12,56.)

Long numbers

We use commas (,) for writing long numbers: thousands and millions:

15,000	fifteen thousand
29,568	twenty-nine thousand, five hundred <u>and</u> sixty-eight (*British English*)

29,568	twenty-nine thousand, five hundred, sixty-eight (*American English*)
250,789	two hundred and fifty thousand, seven hundred <u>and</u> eighty-nine (*British English*)
250,789	two hundred and fifty thousand, seven hundred eighty-nine (*American English*)
5,000,000	five million
£5m	five million pounds
5,000,000,000	five billion
$5.8bn	five point eight billion dollars

8.3 *Currencies*

According to *The Economist* magazine the average price for a McDonald's "Big Mac" hamburger in the USA is $2.51. Can you match the countries, currencies and hamburger prices in other countries?

Country	Currency	Price of a "Big Mac" Hamburger Local currency	Dollars
Japan	Dollar	Real 2.95	1.65
European Union	Rouble	£1.90	3.00
Brazil	Yen	Y294	2.78
Russia	Sterling	€2.56	2.37
United Kingdom	Yuan	$2.51	2.51
China	Real	NT $70.00	2.29
USA	Indonesia	Y 9.90	1.20
Taiwan	Euro	R39.50	1.39
Indonesia	Rupiah	Rp 14,500	1.83

[*Source:* "Big MacCurrencies" © *The Economist Newspaper Limited*, London (27 April, 2000)]

🎧 *Listening*

8.4 *A news broadcast*

Listen to this radio broadcast of the business news and complete the text on page 85.

In the currency markets today the Euro fell against the dollar and sterling. This followed the announcement that Germany would hold a general election in the Autumn. Earlier in the day there were rumours about industrial unrest in France and the threat of more strikes. The euro was adversely affected, losing **(a)** _____ against the US dollar.

British exporters continued to express concern about the growing strength of sterling. British exports were increasingly expensive and uncompetitive overseas, they said. The value of sterling is now up significantly against most major currencies compared with **(b)**___ and **(c)**____ months ago: **(d)**____ against the dollar, **(e)** _____ against the euro, and **(f)**____ against the Japanese yen.

Fast food giant Kentucky Fried Chicken will create **(g)** _____ new jobs over the next five years as part of a large expansion programme in Britain. Over **(h)** _____ new restaurants will open following the chain's **(i)** _____ growth in sales over a five-year period. The announcement followed the opening of KFC's 500th UK outlet in Cardiff, Wales, raising its employment levels to more than 12,000 workers. The company predicts it will have about **(j)** _____ workers in Britain by 2005.

The number of jobless in Germany unexpectedly rose by 12,000 to **(k)** _____ million in March. The German Chancellor has pledged to bring unemployment down to below **(l)** _____ million by 2004.

Language focus

🎧 8.5 *Numbers*

People often have difficulty using numbers. Write out the following numbers in words:

Example:	€368
	You write: *three hundred and sixty-eight euros*
1 3.5%	_____
2 22,000	_____
3 10.5	_____
4 $2.78	_____
5 Y294	_____

6 £1.90 _____
7 9,784,596 _____
8 5,483,495 _____

Reading 1

8.6 McDonald's

Read the following article, which refers to the figures in **8.3** about the price of a "Big Mac" hamburger, and answer the questions below:

McDonald's is the largest food service company in the world. In 1997 world-wide sales exceeded $33 billion and net income was over $1.6 billion. The company has over 23,000 restaurants in 109 countries. Its flagship product is the "Big Mac" hamburger. The Big Mac index was launched about 15 years ago by *The Economist* magazine as a light-hearted guide to the exchange rate between currencies and the cost of living around the world. The first column of the table shows the local currency prices of a Big Mac. The second converts them into dollars: the average price of a Big Mac (including tax) in a typical American city is $2.51. The cheapest hamburger among the countries in the table is in China ($1.20). At the other extreme the most expensive is $3.00 in the United Kingdom. However, there are obvious faults in using this data to compare the cost of living in different countries, e.g. local prices may be affected by trade barriers on meat, sales taxes or significant differences in other items, such as rent.

Match a word or phrase in the text with the following words below:

1 were more than _____
2 the most important _____
3 started _____
4 not serious _____

5 changes _____
6 costly _____
7 information _____

True or false?

a McDonald's has approximately 230 restaurants in each country where it operates.
b *The Economist* created the Big Mac index.
c The cost of living is highest in the UK.

Language focus

8.7 *Making comparisons*

Adjectives

cheap	*cheaper*	*cheapest*
expensive	***more** expensive*	***most** expensive*

The ***cheapest*** hamburger among the countries in the table is in China ($1.20).

One or two syllables	Add *-er* or *-est*	*cheap**er***
One syllable ending with a single consonant	Double the last consonant and add *-er* or *-est*	*bigg**er***
Two syllables ending with -y	Change *y* to *i* and add *-er* or *-est*	*lovel**ier***
Two or more syllables	*more* or *most* before the adjective	***more** expensive*

Other ways to make comparisons:

than	*Computers are cheaper in Hong Kong **than** in France.*
as ... as	*France imports **as** many cars **as** Italy.*

When we say that things are different we use

not as ... as	*France imports cars but **not as** many **as** Britain.*

Practice

A How do these adjectives change when making comparisons?

1 hard _____
2 dear _____
3 efficient _____
4 good _____
5 lucky _____
6 efficient _____
7 interesting _____
8 expensive _____
9 cheap _____
10 costly _____

B Use the appropriate form of the adjectives to complete (**1**) the extract from the radio programme and (**2**) the dialogue below:

(**1**) Cisco Systems, the global Internet specialist, is not only one of the _____ (*big*) companies in the world (based on its market value) but also the _____ (*good*) employer in the United Kingdom. According to a survey carried out by the *Sunday Times* newspaper, its staff are _____ (*happy*) and _____ (*satisfied*) with their work than any other group of employees in the country.

(**2**) **Mark:** Hello. How are you? Haven't seen you for a while. How are things in your new job?
Eloise: Fine, thank you. I like the work. The hours are _____ (*long*) and I have more responsibility now, so it can be very stressful at times. But it's a good career move. The company's one of the _____ (*large*) in the country so there are plenty of opportunities for promotion.
Mark: What are the people like? Is there a good work atmosphere?
Eloise: Most of the employees are _____ (*young*) than me. In fact the boss is only in his mid-thirties.

Reading 2

8.8 Skimming and scanning

Read the following article and answer these questions:

1 Who was responsible for the £32 billion loss?
2 What was the reaction when the trader sold £300 million in shares instead of £3 million?

Two zeros add up to £32 billion loss

A city trader's typing error cost his bosses more than £2 million and led to a £32 billion plunge on the London stock market. By accidentally keying in a couple of extra noughts on his computer screen, the trader sold £300 million of shares instead of the £3 million he meant to.

5

The error, made during share deal in the closing minutes of trading on Monday, caused the FTSE-100 Index to fall 140 points and sparked an inquiry into the safety of the computer system involved.

City trading floors were buzzing with speculation about the identity of
the investment bank and the trader. US firm Lehman Brothers has been   10
linked to the incident but has declined to comment.The trader's bank will
almost certainly have to buy back the shares at higher prices. Analysts
put the losses at about £2 million.

Despite attempts yesterday morning to rectify the situation, the stock
market refused to cancel the trade. A Stock Exchange spokesman said: 15
"We are continuing to speak to the firm in order to investigate how tight
their internal controls are. We expect a certain standard of integrity from
member firms and if we find that adequate controls aren't in place we
have the power to fine them."

The sell order involved a clutch of stocks and sent prices of some of   20
the market's biggest names, including Vodafone and BP, significantly
lower. Henk Potts, of Barclays Stockbrokers, said: "There would have
been a few traders staring in disbelief at their screens for a few minutes."
But, he said, most traders would soon have grasped there had been a
mistake.   25

The Footsie recovered most of the losses, gaining more than 130
points in the first 15 minutes of trading yesterday.

[*Source*: "Two zeros add up to £32 billion loss" by Rebecca Mowling, *Metro*, 16 May 2001]

8.9 *Vocabulary*

Choose the best meaning from **a**, **b** or **c** for each word or expression in
8.8.

1 led to	**a** brought to	
(*lines 1, 2*)	**b** resulted in	
	c followed through	
2 keying (*line 4*)	**a** typing	
	b opening	
	c turning	
3 sparked (*line 7*)	**a** stopped	
	b started	
	c delayed	

4 rectify (*line 14*)	**a** correct	
	b prevent	
	c control	
5 tight (*line16*)	**a** good	
	b helpful	
	c united	
6 integrity	**a** honesty	
(*line 17*)	**b** ability	
	c competence	

7 clutch (*line 20*)   **a** a number
                          b a bag
                          c a small group

8 in disbelief   **a** feeling
   (*line 23*)   incredible
                          b not
                                 believing
                          c in good faith

9 grasped   **a** wondered
   (*line 24*)   **b** understood
                          c said

10 Footsie   **a** FT 100 SE
   (*line 26*)   **b** the Ft
                                 company
                          c Foot group
                                 of companies

8.10 *Comprehension*

Are the following statements true or false?

Read the article in **8.8** again.

a The trader sold too many shares.
b The problem was the result of a computer error.
c Lehman Brothers have admitted it was their mistake.
d The Stock Exchange will fine Vodafone.
e Traders immediately knew that there had been a mistake.
f The Footsie gradually recovered the losses over the next few days.

8.11 *Approximating*

*Analysts put the losses **at about £2million**.*

Match these questions and answers.

1 How long did it take to get there?   **a** *They cost about $450 each.*
2 What time is your meeting?   **b** *I think £1 sterling is worth about US $1.20.*
3 What's the rate at the moment?   **c** *It's round about three o'clock*
4 How much are they?   **d** *About an hour or so.*

Lesson summary

In this lesson you have practised:

● Using figures to discuss currencies and money.
● Extracting information from a radio broadcast.
● Making comparisons between companies.
● Approximating.

Suggestions for further practice

1 Is it possible to buy shares in your company? Look in the financial press and find out the cost of a share.

2 Make a list of statistics about your company. For example, its value, the number of employees, sales. This kind of information may be publicly available in printed form or on the web.

3 Practise listening to numbers in English. For example, listen to the BBC financial news and keep a record of how much your country's currency changes against the dollar in one week.

9 | USING THE TELEPHONE

In this unit you will practise:
- ◆ understanding and using telephone language
- ◆ making offers and requests on the phone
- ◆ making plans and arrangements
- ◆ understanding and leaving voicemail messages

Language:
- ◆ phone numbers
- ◆ the English alphabet and spelling aloud
- ◆ the future tenses

Introduction

9.1 *Telephone questions*

- ● Do you use the telephone a lot?
- ● How often do you use English on the telephone?
- ● What do you find difficult? Understanding the other person? Giving information clearly? Knowing appropriate expressions? Anything else?

🎧 *Listening 1*

9.2 *On the phone*

Christos Georgiou is telephoning the office of Jim Smith. However, Christos is unable to speak to Jim. If possible, listen to the recording first, before you read the conversation below and try to understand why Jim Smith can't talk to Christos Georgiou. Don't worry about trying to understand everything you hear/read.

Secretary	Good morning. Business Travel Limited.
Christos	May I speak to Jim Smith, please?
Secretary	Sorry. His line's busy. Do you want to hold?
Christos	Yes, please.
	(*phone ringing*)
Secretary	Sorry to keep you waiting, caller.
	(*phone ringing*)
Secretary	Sorry. His line's still engaged. Do you want to hold or would you rather leave a message?
Christos	Could you ask him to ring Christos Georgiou from Multimedia Solutions Incorporated on 020 85983? I'll be at this number all morning but I'll be out of the office this afternoon.
Secretary	Sorry. Could you spell the name?
Christos	The first name is C-H-R-I-S-T-O-S. The surname is G-E-O-R-G-I-O-U.
Secretary	Okay. Thank you. I'll make sure he gets your message, Mr Georgiou.
Christos	Thank you. Goodbye.
Secretary	Goodbye.

9.3 *A telephone message*

Jim Smith's secretary puts the note on page 94 on his desk. Compare the note with the phone conversation. There are five errors in the note. Can you find them? Listen to the conversation again if necessary and write your answers below. Then check your answers in the Answer Key.

1 The caller's name is Mr Georgiou, not Mr Christos.

2 ....

3 ....

4 ....

5 ....

Business Travel Ltd
MESSAGE

Day: *Monday*   Date: *14-05*   Time: *11:05* am/pm
To: *Jim Smith*   Extension: *3175*

While you were out...
Mr/Mrs/Ms : *Christos*
Phone number: *020 85993*   Company: *Multimedia*
                                    Solutions Corporation

   called

   came to see you

   will call you back

   call him/her back

   is waiting to see you in...

   has left the following message
He will be in his office this afternoon.

Received by: *Andrea*

9.4 *What would you say?*

1 You are telephoning a client. He picks up the phone and says "Hello".
   What is your reply?
   a Hello. Here is Juan.
   b Hello. I am Juan Garcia.
   c Hello. Juan Garcia speaking.

2 The phone rings. Somebody wants to speak to a colleague who is not
   in the office today. What do you say?
   a I'm sorry. She's not here. Can I take a message?
   b I'm sorry. She's not here. I'm taking a message.
   c I'm sorry. She's not here. Do you like me to write a message?

3 A client you are talking to on the telephone also needs to talk to your colleague Peter Gray in another department. You are going to transfer the call. What do you say?

   a Just hold on and I'll put you across to Peter Gray.

   b Just hold on and I'll put you through to Peter Gray.

   c Just hold on and I'll turn you on to Peter Gray.

4 You're talking to a client but you didn't catch the name of the client's company. What do you say?

   a I didn't catch the name of your company. Can you repeat it , please?

   b Repeat, if you please, the name of your company. I didn't catch it?

   c I didn't catch the name of your company. Repeat it again please.

Language focus

9.5 *Telephone numbers*

> Telephone numbers in English are spoken as separate digits.
>
> | You read/write | You hear/say |
> |---|---|
> | 5980 3761 | *five nine eight zero, ... three seven six one* |
> | 8499 3872 | *eight four double nine, ... three eight seven two* |
> | | OR *eight four nine nine, ... three eight seven two* |

Practice

Listen to these telephone numbers and say them:

a 5599 0921	**d** 8574 0021
b 7846 2254	**e** 8593 0900
c 0466 8777	**f** 3364 0986

9.6 *The alphabet and spelling*

How do you spell your family name? You often need to spell names on the telephone. Do you know how to pronounce the letters of the English alphabet?

It is easy to get confused about the vowel sounds of letters. For example, some people get confused between J and G, or I and E and A. The chart on the next page shows the letters sorted into six groups. All the letters in the same group have the same vowel sound. Listen and try to say them.

AHJK: These all have the /eɪ/ sound.

BCDEGPV: These all contain the /iː/ sound, as in *bee* or *tree*. In American English the last letter of the alphabet is also pronounced like this. Z (zee)

FLMNX: These contain the sound /e/ as in *help* or *red*. In British English, the last letter of the alphabet is pronounced like this. Z (zed)

IY: These contain the /aɪ/ sound as in *try* or *high*.

O: This is the only letter with the /əʊ/ sound as in *boat*.

QUW: These all contain the /uː/ sound as in *blue* or *zoo*.

Here are some more characters in English that sometimes form parts of names and serial numbers that you have to spell out to people.

/ slash or stroke	\ backslash	- dash or hyphen
( ) brackets or parentheses	(open bracket	) close bracket
' apostrophe	@ at	

Don't forget that we say the number 0 in different ways in English:

Zero, O, and *nought* are the most common ones.

When spelling out names and other words which have two letters the same, or reading out numbers, we sometimes say "double" instead of repeating the letter or number, for example:

Little is spelt L-I-double T-L-E (LITTLE).
The telephone number for reservations and tickets is double nine five, three two double seven (9953277).

There are different ways to ask someone how to spell something:

How do you spell your name?
How do you write that?
Can you tell me how to spell that?

 Practice

Practise spelling these names. Say them out loud:

Christos Georgiou   Millennium Systems   Wickham Displays

Your name_____

The name of your company/college_____

Listening 2

 9.7 Voicemail messages

It's particularly important when listening to telephone messages to be able to recognize the letters of the alphabet and numbers.

Jim Smith is checking the messages on his voicemail. Listen and complete the table below.

	Message 1	Message 2	Message 3	Message 4
Name		Liam Dwyer		Yasuko Kitamura
Date				
Dept./Company	Anglo-Spanish Travel Services			
Tel no.				

 9.8 Telephone requests and offers

Match a line from column **A** with a line in column **B** to create mini-dialogues.

Example: 1f.

A	B
1 I'd like to speak to Judy Davies please?	a Go ahead. Dial 9 for an outside line.
2 Can I take a message?	b Certainly. Has he got your number?
3 Could you give him a message?	
4 Would you mind spelling your last name?	c It's M-O-L-E-W-S-K-I.
	d No, that's okay, I'll call again later.
5 Can you tell me when she will be back in the office?	e Of course, sir, no problem.
6 Do you think I could use your phone? I need to contact my office.	f Hold on, I'll put you through.
	g She should be here this afternoon.
7 Could you ask him to give me a call back this afternoon?	

9.9 *In your own language*

Look at these expressions. How would you say them in your language?

1 I'll call/phone/ring you tomorrow. OR I'll give you a call tomorrow.
2 Hello, this is Jim Smith from BTL. OR Jim Smith from BTL speaking.
3 His line is engaged. OR His extension is busy.
4 I'll transfer you to my colleague Michael White. Hold on a minute,
   please. OR I'll put you through to my colleague Michael White. Hold
   on a minute, please.
5 Sorry, could you repeat that? I didn't catch it. OR Sorry, I didn't catch
   your name. Would you mind saying it again?
6 How do you spell that? How do you spell your last name?
7 Can you speak more slowly please? My English isn't all that good.
8 Can you speak a bit louder? OR Can you speak up a little?
9 Would you like to hold, or leave a message?
10 I'll call back later.

🎧 *Listening 3*

9.10 *Second phone call*

Jim Smith from Business Travel Ltd has received the telephone message
from Christos Georgiou. He is telephoning Multimedia Solutions
Incorporated to return Christos Georgiou's call.

If possible, listen to the recording before you read the conversation in
9.12. Don't try to understand everything. Just listen for the answer to this
question:

Question: What was the main problem discussed in the telephone call?

a a problem with MSI's website?
b a delay?
c a mistake with delivery of new software?

🎧 9.11 *Listen for the details*

Answer these **True/False** questions. Circle **T** or **F**. Then listen to the conversation in **9.10** again to check if you were correct.

1 Christos Georgiou is returning John Smith's call.   T / F
2 Christos called Jim Smith earlier.   T / F
3 Jim wanted to tell Christos about a problem.   T / F
4 Multimedia Solutions is designing a new website for
  Business Travel Limited.   T / F
5 The delay will not cause serious problems.   T / F
6 Jim is angry about the delay.   T / F
7 The product will be delivered at the end of next week.   T / F

🎧 9.12 *Second phone call – the script*

Here is the script of the conversation you heard in **9.10**. Fill in the missing words. Then listen to the recording again to check (PA = personal assistant).

PA	Multimedia Solutions Incorporated, Development Section, good morning.
Jim	Oh hello, I'd _____ to speak to Christos Georgiou.
PA	He's on the other line at the moment. I'm his PA. Can I ask who's _____?
Jim	Yes, _____ is Jim Smith from Business Travel Limited. I'm _____ his call from this morning.
PA	Oh yes, Mr Smith. _____ on just a second, I think he's just finished.
Christos	Hello Jim, sorry to _____ you waiting.
Jim	No problem. What's up?
Christos	_____ about the new version of your website. We had some problems with the changes you asked for last week, but it's all _____ out now. However, we are behind schedule and we are not _____ to be able to deliver next week.
Jim	Well, when do you think you will _____ able to deliver?

Christos	We only need two extra days. It'll be _____ for installation by Tuesday of the week after next.
Jim	As long as we get it on the Tuesday there should be no problem. Are you sure there _____ be any more delays?
Christos	Yes, I'm sure.
Jim	Okay, that's fine. But if anything else does come up, please let me _____ as early as possible.
Christos	Of course. If we have any more problems, _____ let you know immediately.
Jim	Thanks a lot. I'll give you a _____ at the end of next week anyway.
Christos	Fine. _____ speak to you then. Have a good weekend.
Jim	Bye.

Practice

Now practise saying the dialogue on your own or with a friend. Look at **Suggestions for further practice** for some other ideas.

Language focus

9.13 Will *and* going to

Look at these four mini-dialogues. Then answer the questions below.

1

2

A The new designs are ready.
B Okay, I'll come and have a look at them this afternoon.

A I'm going to have a look at the new designs.

3  **4**

A I'm flying over to New York next week.
B Oh, really? When are you leaving?
A Monday afternoon.
B How long for?
A I'm coming back on Thursday.

A I've got all these reports to check by Friday. It's impossible.
B I'll give you a hand, if you like.
A That would be great. Will you check the ones from the finance department?

a Which conversations are about plans already made?
b Which conversations are about plans just being made at the moment of speaking?
c Which sentence is an offer to help?
d Which sentence is a request?
e Which conversation is about definite travel arrangements for the near future?

Now complete these grammar rules by matching the phrases on the left with those on the right.

1 We use *will* future
2 We use *going to* + infinitive
3 We use present progressive future
4 We also use *will*

a in offers and requests.
b to talk about definite travel plans in the near future.
c to talk about future plans just as they are being decided.
d to talk about plans already made.

See **Language Reference** for further details.

🎧 9.14 *Further practice of the future*

Choose the best option to complete these dialogues:

1 Any plans for the holidays?
   a Yes, I'm going to go to the USA for a week.
   b Yes, I'm flying to the USA for a week.
   c Yes, I will visit the USA for a week.

2 Your secretary called.
   a Okay, I'm going to call her back.
   b Okay, I'm calling her back.
   c Okay, I'll call her back.

3 How is the new website design coming along?
   a Fine, I think, but I will meet the designers this afternoon.
   b Fine, I think, but I'm going to meet the designers this afternoon.
   c Fine, I think, but I meet the designers this afternoon.

4 Has the company made a decision on the new products yet?
   a Not yet, but we will discuss it in the development meeting on Friday.
   b Not yet, but we are going to discuss it in the development meeting on Friday.

5 **Secretary** I'm afraid Mr Jones isn't in the office this morning. Can I take a message?

   Caller   Yes please. It's Jim Smith from Business Travel Limited. Could you tell him I'll call him tomorrow?

   Secretary a Certainly, Mr Smith. I'm going to give him your message as soon as he arrives.

                  b Certainly, Mr Smith. I'm giving him your message as soon as he arrives.

                  c Certainly, Mr Smith. I'll give him your message as soon as he arrives.

🎧 9.15 *What would you say?*

1 The receptionist tells you there is an English-speaking client on the telephone, then she puts the call through to you. What would you say?

For example, you could say:
Hello, John Clinton here, how can I help you?

2 You telephone a supplier, and they answer the phone like this:
"Comlink Limited, good morning."
You say: ....

3 The person you are visiting tells you that your Managing Director called earlier and wants to talk to you urgently.
You say: ....

4 Someone asks you about your plans for the weekend.
You say: ....

5 You are on a business trip abroad. Someone asks you when you are returning home.
You say: ....

6 You want to know about delivery dates for a product on order.
You say: ....

Some suggested answers have been recorded for you. Listen to check your answers.

Lesson summary

Here are some of the things you practised in this lesson:

● Telephone language:
> *Hello, this is …*
> *I'd like to speak to …*
> *I'll put you through.*
> *The line's engaged/busy. Do you want to hold?*
> *Sorry to keep you waiting.*
> *Can I take a message?*

● Offers and requests:
> *Would you like me to take a message?*
> *Shall I get him to call you back?*
> *I'll tell him you called, if you like.*
> *Do you think I could use your phone?*
> *Would you mind spelling your name again?*
> *Could you ask him to call me back?*

● Talking about future plans:
   We're going to discuss this at tomorrow's meeting.
   I'm flying back on Thursday evening.
   I'll let you know tomorrow.

● Telephone numbers:
   764 1966 "seven six four, one nine six six"
   020 895 4322 "oh two oh, eight nine five, four three double two"

Suggestions for further practice

1 Play the recording without looking at the script. Pause the recording at the end of each line and try to remember what comes next.

2 Write a similar dialogue using your own company's name and products, or changing the situation to something that happened to you recently.

3 Think of other situations where you need to make requests or offers. What would you say?

4 Find a telephone conversation on a British or American video. Write out the conversation and practise it.

5 Practise the dialogues with a friend, first looking at the script, then without looking at the script.

6 Work with a partner. Each writes down 10 telephone numbers. Dictate your numbers to your partner in English.

7 Ask a good English-speaking friend to record telephone messages for you. Listen and write down the messages.

10 | E-COMMERCE

In this unit you will practise:
◆ discussing the role of computers in business
◆ talking about advertising on the Web
◆ giving a presentation

Language:
◆ information technology
◆ presentations: useful expressions
◆ pronunciation: stress

Introduction

10.1 *Are you computer literate?*

● Do you use the Internet in your work?
● What is the difference between the Internet and the Web?
● Do you have an e-mail address?
● Do you know the names of any IT companies? Can you use any software packages?
● Which of the following are famous international IT companies? Cisco systems; Sun; Sony; McDonald's; Ford; Mercedes?

The following terms are used when discussing IT. Can you match the words on the left with their definitions?

software   electronic business, e.g. via the Web
hardware   program which searches through a database
PC   system of interconnected PCs
telemarketing   computing program, e.g. Word, Excel
e-commerce   physical components of computing, e.g. disks
network   selling only via the telephone
search engine   personal computer

🎧 *Listening 1*

10.2 *Computer talk*

Listen to the recording or read these conversations and decide which of the terms described in **10.1** the speakers are talking about.

1 ....

2 ....

3 ....

4 ....

1 A Which would you recommend then?
  B Well, there are a lot of them now on the Web and they can vary in quality a great deal. With the bad ones you can spend ages searching to find what you're looking for. Yahoo is my favourite but I sometimes use Lycos and Altavista too.

2 A Where do you get yours from?
  B A company called Computer Inc. They import the components from the Far East and assemble the PCs and printers here.

3 A Hello. Helpdesk here. Can I help you?
  B Hi. This is Steve Robbins from Marketing. I don't seem able to get access to the customer database. Another person in my department is having the same problem.
  A I'm afraid the whole system is down at the moment. Try again in, say, 15 minutes and hopefully the engineers will have fixed the problem by then.

4 A Thank you for applying for the job and coming to this interview. For the position of administration officer, we are looking for someone who is comfortable using Microsoft Word and Excel.
  B I'm familiar with both. I used them regularly in my last position.

⋒ *Reading*

10.3 *IT and Banking*

How has e-commerce changed business activity? What effect have computerization and the Internet had on the world of commerce?

A Read the article below. What does it say about the impact of new technology on business?

THE IMPACT OF E-COMMERCE ON BANKING

The cost of an ordinary banking transaction in a branch is 100 times that on the Web

Information technology has radically changed the way many industries work. The ability of computers to store and handle information has allowed businesses to get rid of paper records. Computers can store vast amounts of information in a small space, so companies are able to keep much more detailed information about their clients and suppliers. IT has also speeded up the handling of information, so that data can be found easily, sorted instantly and accessed from many different places.

The Internet and e-mail have revolutionized business communication. Intranets allow employees to 'talk' to each other, to distribute memos and to access company documents and databases without moving from their desks. The Internet allows business people to access all kinds of essential information and to communicate almost instantly with clients, suppliers and other contacts.

Within the traditional banking sector, electronic commerce has brought about radical change. The high-speed transfer of information has allowed customers to access their accounts through ATMs (Automatic Teller Machines) – also known as 'hole-in-the-wall' banking machines. Customers not only withdraw money from wherever they are, they can also check their account balances, order a statement and even print out a mini-statement of their banking records. One of the major reasons banks have encouraged the greater use of technology is cost efficiency. The cost of an ordinary banking transaction in a branch is 100 times greater than that on the Web (Digital Britain 1999 Microsoft limited). With online banking, customers can access their account from their home or office PCs and carry out banking business without ever going near a 'real' bank. As a result banks need fewer branches and fewer employees to deal with customers' needs.

B Now read the article again and answer these questions:

1 How much cheaper is it to carry out a transaction on the Internet than in a branch?

2 Complete the following table:

The impact of e-commerce on banking	
Advantages	**Disadvantages**
_____	_____
_____	_____
_____	_____
_____	_____
_____	_____

10.4 *Vocabulary – Word partnerships*

A Join together words from each column to make word partnerships.

Example: 1e

1	service	**a**	records
2	information	**b**	changes
3	paper	**c**	technology
4	radical	**d**	information
5	essential	**e**	industries

B Now complete these sentences using one of the word partnerships in **A**.

1 The computer system is not working again. Fortunately we have _____ _____ of the data you require.

2 The impact of _____ _____ has caused the banking industry to experience enormous changes in recent years.

3 One result of the _____ _____ in banking has been the redundancy of large numbers of staff.

4 In certain parts of the country as much as 70 per cent of the workforce are now employed in the _____ _____.

5 _____ _____, such as clients' details, are kept on a database in the marketing office.

Language focus

10.5 *Pronunciation – Stress*

When we speak the emphasis we give to a particular syllable in a word is called stress. For example the stress in *number* is on the first syllable. In the word *advise* it is on the second syllable.

Dictionaries usually indicate the pronunciation of a word using phonetic symbols, e.g. /'simbəl/. However, if you do not know phonetics, you can still work out the stress. Normally, there is a ' symbol (e.g. /'nʌmbə/, /əd'vaɪz/) before the stressed syllable.

A Listen and repeat the following words, in particular noting the stress.

B Listen again and mark the stress. The first one has been done as an example:

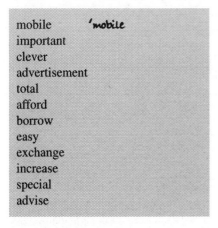

mobile   'mobile
important
clever
advertisement
total
afford
borrow
easy
exchange
increase
special
advise

🎧 *Listening 2*

10.6 *Advertising online*

A Pre-listening questions: It is now possible to buy everything from books and CDs to airline tickets and house insurance on the Web. Most business people believe that buying and selling online will become increasingly important.

- Have you ever bought something online?
- Does your company advertise online?
- Have you seen adverts on the Web? Do you think they are effective?

B Listen to Wang Yi, an IT consultant. Make notes as you listen. How many different types of advertising methods does she discuss?

Wang Yi	Well, the most popular form of Web advertising is the banner ad. These appear as a rectangular block which flashes or moves on the screen trying to attract your attention. In my opinion they don't achieve very much. Most people just ignore them. The bottom line is that people simply do not click on ads.
Peter Blake	So they are a waste of money?
Wang Yi	In my opinion, yes, I think so. However, I know others take a different view and feel that if the ad is compelling enough it can reinforce the company's brand in the consumer's mind. But, personally I'm not convinced it's worth the money.
Peter Blake	What other forms of advertising are there?
Wang Yi	Classified advertising has better results than banners.
Peter Blake	With classifieds you pay to have your product or service listed in specific categories, don't you?
Wang Yi	Yes, that's it. The same as the classified ads in the newspaper.
Peter Blake	I guess it's probably more successful because users are searching for a specific item, such as accommodation, a builder or whatever.
Wang Yi	Yes. What is more, it can suit all budgets. Also, it's sometimes possible to get a free basic listing and then to upgrade to include hyperlinks and email enquiry forms.
Peter Blake	Anything else worth considering?
Wang Yi	I would recommend e-zines.
Peter Blake	These are electronic magazines?
Wang Yi	That's right. An advert in an appropriate e-zine can be a highly effective form of promotion. If the marketing message is sufficiently targeted to its audience, then it is estimated that as many as one in five users will click

through your website. This compares with the average click rate of between 0.3 and 0.1 per cent for the banner advertising.

Comprehension

1 Which is the most successful kind of advertising on the Web? Why?
2 Which method of advertising would you use if you didn't have much money to spend?
3 Which is the least successful way of advertising?
4 You are also at this meeting on advertising on the Web. What questions would you ask?

🎧 Listening 3

10.7 Preparing a presentation

A Can you think of a person, famous or perhaps someone you know at work, who is a good public speaker? Nelson Mandela? The American President? The president of your country? What are the qualities of a good speaker? Which of the following are important? not very important? unhelpful?

	important	not very important	unhelpful
appear confident	✔		
to speak loudly and slowly			
lots of good jokes			
give detailed information			
use visual aids			
read your presentation from your notes			
knowledge of the audience			

B Roberto Diaz is going to give a presentation on Web advertising. Although he knows a lot about the topic he doesn't feel confident about his presentation skills and has asked a colleague, Paulo Gonzalez, to advise. Listen to the two versions of the start of Roberto's presentation, one before and one after receiving advice. Which one is better and why ?

Introduction 1:

Good morning everybody. My name is Roberto Diaz from Webmaster Incorporated and I'm very pleased to be here today to talk to you about starting up online advertising. The presentation will be divided into two parts. I'd like to start by offering some general guidelines concerning online advertising, then I will discuss the costs involved and finally my recommendations for your company. Of course, I will be happy to answer any questions either during or at the end of the presentation.

Introduction 2:

Hi everybody. My company, Webmaster Incorporated, sent me here to talk about online advertising. I believe you're thinking about doing some advertising on the Web. Basically, I'm going to talk about the kind of work I do at Webmaster and you can ask questions. I don't know if I'll be able to answer them but I'll try.

C Listen to the recording or read the dialogue between Paulo and Roberto. What advice does Paulo give for the following:

1 the introduction

2 the main body of the presentation

3 the conclusion

Paulo	Well, most people are nervous when giving a presentation. And some find it more difficult to speak in public than others. However, there are certain things you can do to make sure that your presentation is effective. Find out about the audience. How much do they know about the subject? I think your audience for this talk know very little about on-line advertising so you will have to include some basic information about doing business on the web. Also, check out the location. You will feel more comfortable if you know what the room will be like. Will it be here at Webmaster or is the presentation elsewhere?
Roberto	It's in the conference room upstairs.
Paulo	Fine. You should separate the presentation into three parts: introduction, main body and conclusion. In the introduction you introduce yourself, the purpose of the presentation and say how you will organize things... you know... something like... first, I'm going to discuss this, then I'll talk about that... and so on. Oh, and say whether you want the audience to ask questions during or at the end of the presentation. I put a lot of time and effort into getting the introduction right. Usually I memorize the words of the introduction just like an actor does with a script. First impressions are very important. Then, in the main part of the presentation clearly signal each of the points. I use Microsoft Powerpoint and have each main point displayed on an overhead screen. Finally, in the conclusion a brief summary, thank them for their attention and ask again about questions.
Roberto	You make it sound easy.
Paulo	Well, it isn't. But if you spend some time preparing yourself I'm sure you will be fine.

Language focus

10.8 *Useful phrases for presentations*

Here are some useful expressions for making an effective presentation:

Introducing yourself:

> *Good Afternoon. My name is Paulo Diaz and I'm the Marketing Director at Webmaster Inc.*
>
> *Hello. I'm Paulo Diaz and on behalf of Webmaster Inc I'd like to welcome you to today's presentation.*

Telling the audience about the structure of your presentation:

> *My talk will be divided into five parts. Part one will deal with ... and part two ...*
>
> *First of all, I'm going to look at ... Then ...*

Introducing the first point:

> *I'd like to begin by discussing ...*
>
> *To start with, I'd like to consider ...*

Starting a new point:

> *Moving on ...*
>
> *Next ...*

Referring to a previous point:

> *As I said before ...*
>
> *In part one of my talk I mentioned ...*

Concluding:

> *That brings me to the end of my presentation. Thank you for your attention.*
>
> *That concludes my talk. Thank you very much.*

Inviting questions:

> *Are there any questions?*
>
> *If you have any questions, I will be glad to answer them.*

Under which of the above headings would you put the following expressions?

1 That covers everything I wanted to say.

2 Next we come to ...

3 Let me introduce myself.

4 So, to summarize ...

5 As I said previously ...

6 I'd like to conclude here.

🎧 *Listening 4*

10.9 *The presentation*

Listen to Roberto's practice presentation.

1 How many of the expressions in **10.8** does he use?

2 Does he follow Paulo's advice?

Hello. I'm Roberto Diaz, Marketing Director of Webmaster Inc and on behalf of the company I'd like to welcome you to this presentation about online advertising. This is a new, exciting and powerful way of increasing your company's presence in the market-place and today I want to offer some general guidelines.

To start with, you should do some research and make a list of those websites that sell advertising space and therefore are likely to attract your target customer. For example, a travel agent might advertise on the National Tourist Organization website.

Secondly, some sites are much more popular than others, so find out how many people visit the site. For e-zine advertising you should find out the number of subscribers your message will be going to. The owners of the site should be able to provide these statistics, called 'site demographics'.

Thirdly, think carefully about which page on your website you'd like to send visitors to. For large organizations the home page is hardly ever the best place. However, if it's a product information page or an enquiry from deep within your site you need to ensure that this page has sufficient links for the user to be able to continue navigating. If there is a danger that your visitors will get lost, then consider designing a 'bridging' page to welcome visitors from your adverts.

Fourthly, having an e-mail enquiry form on another website is an efficient way to capture new enquirers if the e-mail is set up to go to the right person. This may seem obvious but it can be a problem in large organizations with centralized marketing departments. Whose responsibility is it to respond? Is it policy to acknowledge enquiries within a specified time limit?

After a set period – say, three months – results can be measured in terms of an increase in the number of visitors to your site (which is good); an increase in the number of e-mail enquiries received (which is better); an increase in the number of products/services bought (which is best of all).

A regular analysis of these figures against your expenditure on marketing will help you calculate the return on your investment. Online advertising is simply a way to get surfers to the right part of your website more quickly, ensuring that their expectations are fulfilled...

...Well, that brings me to the end of my presentation. If you have any questions I will be happy to answer them.

[*Source*: "A look at the most effective options available to online advertisers" by Fiona Joseph, *EL Gazette*, June 2001]

10.10 *Prepare a short presentation*

Try to prepare your own presentation using the following information:

Subject: Your job and your ambitions.

Audience: Your old school has invited past students to talk about their work to those currently in the final year of their school education.

Main body: Qualifications and skills needed/responsibilities of the job/ advantages and disadvantages/career future.

Record your presentation on cassette or, even better, on a video tape. When you have practised your presentation think about these questions.

1 What do you think someone listening to your presentation would say about it and why? What were the strengths of the presentation?
2 Did you keep to your time limit? If not, why?
3 Do you feel the presentation was well-organized? For example, did you indicate clearly when you were moving to another point?
4 Did you have any visual materials, such as drawings or plans, to help illustrate your talk?
5 What questions do you think the audience might ask? Do you have answers for these questions?
6 If possible, ask a friend who speaks English to watch your presentation and comment on the delivery, e.g. was your voice loud enough? Did you speak too quickly or too slowly? Could you remember what to say or did you keep looking at your notes?
7 When you do the presentation again how will you do it differently?

(See also **Useful Web Addresses** on page 229.)

11 | SOCIALIZING

In this unit you will practise:
◆ making and responding to invitations
◆ social conversations with business contacts
◆ entertaining business clients (in a restaurant and in a bar)

Language:
◆ accepting and declining invitations
◆ small talk
◆ business idioms
◆ formality
◆ polite requests

🎧 Listening 1

11.1 *Invitations*

Establishing good personal relations can be very important for success in business. Consequently, entertaining clients and socializing with prospective business partners is an regular part of commercial life. A lot of business deals take place outside the company office, in conversations in a bar or during a meal at a restaurant.

Michael Blythe works for an international accounting firm and his job frequently includes entertaining foreign clients. You are going to hear extracts from two telephone conversations involving Michael Blythe.

1 In which dialogue is Michael Blythe's invitation to go for a meal accepted?
2 In which dialogue is Michael Blythe talking to someone he already knows?
3 Listen to the dialogues again and fill in the missing words on the next page.

Dialogue 1

Michael Blythe	Hi Faisal. Good to talk to you again. How are you?
Faisal Ali	Fine, thanks Michael. How are you?
Michael Blythe	Very good, thanks.
Faisal Ali	Can you remind me about the timetable on Friday when I'm coming to your office?
Michael Blythe	We're meeting Peter Bowles, the marketing manager, at 2 pm and then Fred Johnson, the general manager, will join us at 4 pm. I think you met Fred when you were here last time but you won't have met Peter before as he only started here a couple of months ago.
Faisal Ali	That's fine. I look forward to meeting them. So, do you think we will we be able to get everything sorted out by the end of the day?
Michael Blythe	Yes, sure. We should be finished by 5 pm.
Faisal Ali	Great.
Michael Blythe	Faisal, would you be free before 2 pm? _____ first for lunch, say at 12.00? We could go to a local restaurant just near our offices.
Faisal Ali	Yes. _____. Shall I meet you at, say 11.50, in the foyer of your office block?

Dialogue 2

Andrea Hall	Hello. Andrea Hall here.
Michael Blythe	Good morning Ms Hall. Michael Blythe here from Wisbech International.
Andrea Hall	Oh hello. Mr Blythe.
Michael Blythe	I'm ringing in connection with the arrangements for your visit to our offices later this week. We had arranged to have the meeting on Friday afternoon, probably finishing around 5 pm. And _____ you and your colleagues would let us take you to dinner afterwards.

Andrea Hall	_____. I'm afraid I will have to say no. Unfortunately our flight back to Glasgow leaves at 6.30 so I doubt if there will be enough time for a meal. However, we could perhaps go for a drink if there's a suitable bar near your offices?
Michael Blythe	Yes. We're in the centre of town so there are lots ...

Language focus

🎧 11.2 *Accepting and declining*

Inviting

(a new business client)

> *We were wondering if you and your colleagues would let us take you to dinner?*
> *Would you care to join us for dinner?*
> *We would like to invite you to dinner.*

(someone you know well)

> *How about dinner later on?*
> *Why not join us for dinner later?*
> *Do you fancy a drink later?*

Accepting invitations

(a new business contact)

> *Thank you very much. That would be nice.*
> *Thank you. I'd be delighted to join you.*

(less formal, someone you know)

> *Thanks. A good idea.*
> *Thanks. Great.*

Refusing an invitation

(a new business contact)

> *Thank you for inviting me. Unfortunately I have a prior engagement. Maybe we could arrange something for another time?*
> *That's very kind of you. However, I'm afraid I have another commitment on Friday evening.*

(less formal, someone you know)
Thanks. But, I'm sorry. I can't that particular evening. Another time perhaps?

🎧 *Listening 2*

11.3 *More invitations*

Listen to the recording. Respond to the invitations using the expressions given in **11.2**.

a Accept the invitation.
b Decline the invitation.
c Accept the invitation.

a If you're free later this evening, we were wondering if you would like to meet us for a drink?

b As it's your first time in Minsk, I would be happy to show you round the city's main sites. Would you be interested?

c Do you play golf? There is a fabulous course on the outskirts of the city. If you like, we could arrange to play a few rounds at the weekend.

🎧 *Listening 3*

11.4 *New contacts and old friends (formality)*

You will hear two conversations. Read the information given below about the speakers. What differences would you expect to hear in a conversation between business people who know each other well and people who meet for the first time?

Conversation A

Anna Smith is part of a British Government trade delegation to South Korea. After the official speeches are over she attends a cocktail reception where the delegates have a chance to socialize and to network. She is introduced to Mr Sang Hoon.

Conference Organizer	May I introduce Mr Sang Hoon?
Sang Hoon	How do you do Ms Smith?
Anna Smith	How do you do?
Sang Hoon	I enjoyed your presentation very much.
Anna Smith	Thank you.
Sang Hoon	May I give you my card? My name is Mr Sang Hoon from *Dysanne* Engineering plant.
Anna Smith	Thank you. And here's mine. My apologies again for arriving a little late this morning at the presentation and keeping you all waiting. The plane into Seoul was delayed by bad weather.
Sang Hoon	Oh, not at all. That's quite all right. Would you care for a cigarette?
Anna Smith	No thank you. I gave up a couple of years ago.
Sang Hoon	Is this your first visit to Korea, Ms Smith?

Conversation B

Mark Greenspan from New York and Julio da Silva from Mexico City have done business together many times. Julio is visiting New York and has arranged to meet Mark in a bar in the evening.

Mark Greenspan	Hi Julio. Good to see you again.
Julio da Silva	Mark! Hello. How are you?
Mark Greenspan	Sorry I'm late.
Julio da Silva	Oh, that's okay.
Mark Greenspan	I'm fine, thanks. How are things in Mexico City? How's business?
Julio da Silva	Good. Very good in fact. There's talk of expansion and opening new offices in Acapulco.
Mark Greenspan	Really! Let me get you a drink and then you can tell me all about it. What would you like? A beer?
Julio da Silva	Yeah. That'd be great. Is it okay to smoke in here?
Mark Greenspan	Go ahead. We're in the smoking area.

Julio da Silva	Thanks. Well, cheers!
Mark Greenspan	Cheers, Julio. How's the family?
Julio da Silva	They're great. Maria sends her regards. How are your kids getting on?
Mark Greenspan	Oh, pretty much the same as usual. So tell me about these expansion plans.
Julio da Silva	Well, they're already pretty far advanced. We're hoping to get the green light this month to rent the place in Acapulco.
Mark Greenspan	Who's going to be working down there?
Julio da Silva	I think Juan has got it all sewn up. It was his baby in the first place.

Comprehension

1 Who smokes?
2 Who has just given a presentation?
3 Where does Julio work?
4 What did Sang Hoon give to Anna Smith ?
5 What did Mark offer Julio?

Note:

1 'How do you do?' is only used when you meet someone for the first time. Also, it is not really a question but a formal way to say Hello.
2 'How are you?' is a question and requires an answer. 'Fine, thanks'.

Language focus

11.5 *Small talk*

"Small talk" describes the remarks we make to friends and people we meet to start a conversation or just to be friendly. In English-speaking countries we often use topics such as the weather or sports for small talk.

A What would you say?

a It's the start of the week and you meet a colleague on the way into the office.
b You are meeting a regular client who is also a keen golfer.
c A supplier has just given you a small gift.
d You are in the lift in your office building. A colleague, who you haven't seen for a while, gets in the lift too.

e You are meeting a client at the airport and then taking him to your offices for a meeting. As you haven't met before, you don't know what he looks like but you see someone who could be him.

B Match the situations (**a–e**) above with one or more of the following remarks:

1 How was your weekend?

2 Was the journey all right?

3 Have you played much lately?

4 That's very kind of you.

5 Hello, Peter. How are things in the IT section?

6 Excuse me. Are you Mr Andrews? I'm ... from MS Development.

7 Did you watch the football yesterday?

8 Great weather we are having at the moment.

9 I'm afraid the weather hasn't been very good recently.

11.6 *Business idioms*

In less formal settings people tend to use more idiomatic language. Idioms can be difficult to use appropriately and successfully in conversation. So, be warned! However, it is useful to be familiar with some expressions so that you can understand what people are talking about.

A The following are idioms that you might hear in a business context. Match the idioms on the left with their explanation on the right.

1 to get the green light	**a**	to be very busy
2 red tape	**b**	a plan which will probably not succeed
3 to put on hold	**c**	to start something happening
4 in the pipeline	**d**	official rules that seem unnecessary and
5 on the blink		cause delay
6 to start the ball rolling	**e**	in debt
7 to be tied up	**f**	to receive permission or approval to proceed
8 in the red	**g**	not working properly
9 a long shot	**h**	planned for the near future
	i	decide not to continue for a while

B Fill the gaps using one of the above idioms. You may have to adapt them to fit the context.

1 We've _____ _____ _____ _____ to go ahead with the project.

2 It's taking such a long time to finalize the deal. It's because of all the government _____ _____ .

3 The decision has been _____ _____ _____ until the end of the year.

4 We've got a new website ____ _____ _____ for next May.

5 I'm afraid I can't give you the exact figures right now. The computer network has been ____ _____ _____ all morning.

6 Webmaster Inc. _____ _____ _____ _____ when they reduced their prices by 10 per cent. All the other computer hardware companies were forced to do the same.

7 Let me look at my diary. I'm afraid I don't have any free time on Thursday. I'm _____ ____ all day.

8 This is a statement from the bank. As you know we've been overdrawn for the past two months. This situation hasn't changed. We're still ____ _____ _____.

9 It's ____ _____ _____ but we're so desperate I'm willing to try anything.

11.7 *Entertaining in a restaurant*

A Business meetings often continue in social situations such as in a restaurant or a bar.

Can you match the food with the country?

Food	Country
curry	Mexico
pate	Italy
spaghetti bolognaise	India
borscht	Tunisia
tacos	Russia
couscous	Japan
sushi	France

B Here are descriptions of two of the dishes above. Which ones?

1 In Britain it's now more popular than fish and chips. There are many varieties, some are very hot and spicy and others quite mild.

2 It looks rather like a plateful of string covered in meat and tomatoes.

3 What is a typical dish from your country? How would you describe this to a visitor?

Vocabulary: *It's rather spicy...*
            It's a bit like... / It's rather like...
            It's the speciality of this region/restaurant

4 An important client is visiting your company and you have the responsibility of choosing a restaurant and deciding on the meal. Write down the menu.

🎧 11.8 *Entertaining in a bar*

Match the requests on the left with the answers on the right.

What would you like to drink?	I'd better not. I'm driving.
	Thanks all the same.
What kind of wine would you like?	Cheers.
This is on me./It's my round.	A pint of Guinness, please.
Cheers.	A dry white wine, please.
Another one before you go?	Thank you very much.

🎧 *Listening 4*

11.9 *Polite requests*

What would you say?

A What would you say if you are in a bar with some new business contacts who are being very generous and they insist on buying you more drinks than you want. You do not want to get drunk but you are keen not to offend your hosts.

B You have been invited to the home of an important client. It's getting late. You are keen to leave and return to your hotel room to do some work to prepare for the meeting tomorrow. Your host then brings out his holiday photographs to show you.

C Listen to the dialogues and note down the language used for asking questions politely.

Asking questions politely	Answer: Yes	Answer: No
1 Excuse me, Could you...?	Certainly	
2 Is it alright to...?		Sorry. I'm afraid ...
3 Do you mind if...	Please do	
4		
5		
6		
7		
8		

1 Excuse me, could you tell Ms Chin that Linda Scott is here to see her?
Certainly. Please take a seat while I contact her office.

2 Is it all right to smoke in here?
Sorry, I'm afraid it isn't. This is a no-smoking area.

3 Do you mind if I open the window for a minute? It's a bit stuffy in here.
Please do.

4 Sorry to disturb you. Can I get my coat?
Yes, of course. Sorry, I didn't realize I was in the way.

5 Could I have a glass of water, please?
Here you are.

6 May I use your phone to make a quick call to the office?
Yes. Please help yourself.

7 Would you like some coffee while you're waiting?
That would be lovely. Thank you.

8 Could you tell me where the toilet is, please?
Sorry. I'm a visitor here.

Practice

What would you say to make the following more polite? Listen to the recording for some suggestions.

a Put your coat there.
b Coffee?
c How do you spell your name?
d What company are you from?
e What do you want?
f Where can I smoke?

Listening 5

11.10 Intonation and politeness

It is not only the words you use that make a request polite. Intonation is very important too.

A Listen to these two versions of the same sentence. In the first version the speaker is angry and in the second version the speaker is polite. Can you hear the difference? Listen again and try to copy the speaker:

Could you sort out this problem by tomorrow?

B You will hear two versions of each request. Decide which is the more polite version **a** or **b**?

1 I have been waiting over half an hour now. How much longer do you think it will be before I can see Mr Jameson?

2 Could I have the bill, please?

3 Excuse me. What did you say?

Lesson summary

Here are some of the things you practised in this lesson:

- Invitations:
  Would you care to join us for dinner?
  Thank you. I'd be delighted to join you.
  Thank you for inviting me. Unfortunately I have a prior engagement.
  Maybe we could arrange something for another time?

- Formality:
  Would you care for a cigarette?
  That would be great.

- Small talk:
  Did you have a pleasant flight?

- Business idioms:
  The computer's on the blink.

- Entertaining:
  It's the speciality of this region.
  This is on me.
  Just a soft drink for me.

- Polite requests:
  May I use your phone to make a quick call to the office?

Suggestions for further practice

Two of your company's important business clients (one male and one female, both aged about 35) will be visiting your city for the first time. Plan a weekend's entertainment for them.

12 MAKING CONTACT

In this unit you will practise:
♦ making an enquiry about the services a company offers
♦ describing your company and saying what it does
♦ talking about requirements and abilities
♦ exchanging contact details and suggesting further meetings

Language:
♦ business sectors and activities
♦ capability
♦ polite requests and offers

Introduction

12.1 *Attracting the customers*

Think of the company you work for or another company you know about.

● What products and/or services does the company provide?

● Who buys these products/services? Is it private individuals, other companies, government organizations?

● How do potential customers find out about the company? Tick all the ones that apply, and write any more ideas you can think of.

    1 Advertisements in the media (television, radio, newspapers and magazines).

    2 Advertisements and features in trade journals.

    3 Trade fairs.

    4 Listing in directories (such as Yellow Pages).

    5 Web pages on the Internet.

    6 Direct mailing to potential customers.

● What publicity material is given to customers who contact your company to make an enquiry?

🎧 *Listening 1*

12.2 *Making an enquiry about a company*

Jim Smith is at an e-commerce business exhibition. He is talking to the representative from an Internet design company. Read the questions then listen to (or read) the conversation to find the answers.

1 Who does Jim Smith work for?
2 Why is he at the exhibition?
3 What does Mike Saunders give Jim?
4 What do you think Jim is going to do after the conference?
   a Have dinner with Mike Saunders.
   b Look at some of the websites designed by Mike Saunders's company.
   c Write a letter to Mike Saunders offering him a job.
   d Arrange a meeting with Mike Saunders.

Mike	Good morning
Jim	Hello there. Do you have any more information about the services you provide? A brochure or something?
Mike	Yes sure. Here you go. This tells you quite a lot about us. There are some contact details inside as well. What exactly is it you are looking for?
Jim	Oh, well we are looking to expand the capabilities of our website, and I am trying to find out what sort of support we can get from specialized companies.
Mike	We have some brochures here about the kinds of services we offer. What area are you in?
Jim	Travel. I don't know if you have heard of us, Business Travel Limited. My name's Jim Smith.
Mike	Mike Saunders. Here's my card.
Jim	Thanks very much.
Mike	Basically we can provide help at different levels – from providing consultancy and advice to setting up, running and maintaining a fully interactive e-commerce site. What sort of services are you looking for?
Jim	Well, actually we already have a website that basically just

gives information for our clients. We also use the Internet to book flights directly from the airlines, and the same sort of thing with the hotels. But now we would like to allow our clients to access our services directly for themselves. Online booking and so on.

Mike   Right, well, I'm sure we can help. We have already set up interactive sites with full e-commerce capability for a number of clients. There is a list of our websites on the back of this brochure. You might like to take a look at some of these sites.

Jim   Thanks. I'll take a look. I'll be in touch.

Mike   Okay, that's fine. Goodbye.

12.3 *Listen for the details*

True or false? Write **T** or **F** next to the statements below to show if they are True or False.

1 Jim Smith has met Mike Saunders before. *F*
2 BTL already has a website.
3 Jim Smith is interested in getting a specialist company to develop BTL's website.
4 Jim gave Mike his business card and a brochure about BTL.
5 Mike Saunders's company has never designed e-commerce sites before.
6 Jim thinks Mike Saunders's company might be able to help BTL.
7 Jim suggested that Mike should look at BTL's website.

Language focus

12.4 *Making enquiries*

Here is some useful language for making an enquiry about a company:

Can you tell me a bit more about your company/about the services you offer?
I'd like some more information about your products.
Do you have a brochure or something with some more information?
What areas do you specialize in?
Where are you based?

> *How long have you been doing this kind of work?*
> *Can you give me some idea about prices?*

This language is useful for dealing with enquiries:

> *What area are you in?*
> *What exactly are you looking for?*
> *This brochure gives information about our services and costs.*
> *Here's my card. You can call me on this number.*
> *If you could give me your contact details, I'll get back to you/I'll send you some more information.*
> *Would you like me to ask our sales manager to get in touch with you?*

12.5 *You make an enquiry*

You are at a trade fair. You see that one of the exhibitors is offering a product (or service) you are interested in.

1 Decide what the product/service is and write a list of possible questions about it.
2 Write and/or record the conversation between yourself and the representative of the company. If you like, you can imagine that the person you are talking to is helpful, unfriendly, polite, enthusiastic about his products, etc.
3 Replay the recording or review the written conversation. See if you can improve it in some way.

🎧 *Listening 2*

12.6 *Making contact by phone*

Mike Saunders is calling a recruitment agency. He needs some temporary staff to work on an IT project. There are some words missing from the conversation. Try to fill in the missing words, then listen to the conversation to check your answers. If you need extra help, choose the words from the box below.

Receptionist	Project Personnel, good morning.
Mike	Oh good morning, I want to talk to someone about getting some IT consultants in, on a temporary basis.
Receptionist	I'll put you _____ to our IT department. Hold on a minute.

Celia	IT recruitment. Celia Robins _____.
Mike	Oh, good morning. My name is Mike Saunders, I work with a company called Multimedia Solutions. I don't think we have used your agency before.
Celia	How can I _____ you Mr Saunders?
Mike	We need to recruit extra web designers for a new contract. The project will probably _____ about one and a half to two months.
Celia	Right. How _____ people are we talking about exactly?
Mike	Five. We need people with _____ in e-commerce, using Dreamweaver and Oracle database. Do you have anyone like that?
Celia	Yes, that should be no problem. When do you _____ them for?
Mike	As soon as _____. Say next week? I know that is short notice but we need to get them in pretty urgently.
Celia	Okay. We do have some suitable people, I need to check if they are _____ for starting next week. I could fax or e-mail some CVs over to you this afternoon.
Mike	That would be great. Can you give me some _____ about cost?
Celia	If you need people for more than a month, around £50 an hour.
Mike	Right. Well if you have _____ people that would be fine.
Celia	Okay, well _____ it with me and as I say I should be able to send you the details this afternoon.
Mike	Okay, I'll _____ you my e-mail. It's M dot Saunders S-A-U-N-D-E-R-S at M-S-I dot co dot U-K. And the phone number is 020 7648 6868.
Celia	Fine. I'll be in _____ this afternoon.

available	experience	give	help	leave
idea	need	speaking	suitable	take/last
through	touch	many	possible	

Language focus

🎧 12.7 *Polite requests and offers*

There are a number of ways to be polite when you are asking for help, or when you need other people to do something for you. In English it is common to use this polite language even if you are asking for something routine.

- Make the request a question, using *would you...?, could you...?, will you...?* or *can you...?*:

  Can you give me a brochure about your products?
  Could you tell me a little more about the services you offer?

- Add *please* usually at the beginning or end of the sentence.

  Can you tell me your name, please? (on the phone, to a caller)
  Please could you despatch the order as soon as possible as it is required urgently? (in an order letter)

- Use some of these expressions:

  Could you possibly ...;
  I would be grateful if you could ... (very formal, usually in written English);
  Would you mind ...ing ...?
  I was wondering if you could ...

  Could you possibly send us five copies of your catalogue?
  I was wondering if you could come and talk to our MD about this new system.
  Would you mind faxing over a price list this afternoon?
  We would be grateful if you could give us a breakdown of costs as soon as possible.

- When you are offering to do something for someone else the following expressions are useful:

  Can I help you?
  Would you like us to quote for different quantities?
  I'll send over the specifications this afternoon, if you like.
  Let me give you a catalogue. It contains all our products and prices.

🎧 Practice

Complete these mini-conversations with one of the expressions in the box below, then listen to the recording to check your answers.

1 Could you tell me the times of flights to Frankfurt, please?

2 Mrs Williams will be down in five minutes. Would you like me to get you a coffee or something?

3 Would you mind sending us two extra copies of your price list, please?

4 I'm arriving in Munich tomorrow at 10 in the morning.

5 We are very interested in your new software, but I was wondering if you could come here and give a demonstration to our finance department.

6 Do you think you could send some more information about the new light bulbs? Specifications and prices, etc.?

---

a Certainly sir. When do you want to fly?

b No problem. I'll put them in the post today.

c Yes please. Black coffee with two sugars, please.

d Okay, that's fine, I'll send a car to the airport to meet you, if you like.

e Of course, that would be no problem. When would you like me to come?

f Of course. Would you like us to send you a sample as well?

Now choose one of the conversations and extend it to make a complete conversation.

Example:

Good morning. Business Travel Limited. How can I help you?

Can you tell me the times of flights to Munich?

Certainly sir. When do you want to fly?

Well, leaving London around 10 tomorrow morning. I have to arrive before lunchtime.

Okay, well there is a flight with Lufthansa at 9.45. That arrives in Munich at 12 exactly. And there is a British Airways flight at 10.05, which gets into Munich at 12.30.

I'll take the British Airways flight then. I need two tickets, business class, coming back the following day around the same time. *etc.*

🎧 12.8 *Saying what your company can do*

Listen to the mini conversations and texts and fill in the missing words below.

1 Are you _____ _____ supply 200 units from stock?
   Yes, I think we _____ _____ that. Let me just check on the computer.

2 The new machine is _____ _____ producing 75 copies a minute. And it _____ _____ programmed for double-sided, sorting, stapling and hole punching _____ _____ 100 sheets at a time.

3 Do you have any _____ _____ supplying personnel for overseas assignments?
   Oh, yes, we _____ _____ dealt with a number of overseas placements.

4 Would it _____ _____ to deliver our order before the end of this month?
   Yes of course. We _____ _____ delivery within two weeks.

can do	able to	can guarantee	capable of
experience of		can be	have already
	be possible	up to	

12.9 *Talking about your company*

How would you handle an enquiry about your company? Think about some of the questions you might get asked by someone who is interested in your company's products or services. (If you are not working for anyone at the moment, think of a company you know well). Write a telephone conversation between yourself and a customer. Include offers and requests, and questions about your company's capabilities and experience.

If possible, record the conversation. Then review your work and think about ways to improve it.

🎧 *Listening 3*

12.10 *Starting a conversation*

Peter and Geoff are at a conference. They do not know each other, but they have been sitting together during a talk.

Listen to (or read) the conversation and answer these questions.

1 Who does Peter work for?
2 What services does his company provide?
3 Who does Geoff work for?
4 What is his job?
5 What do they both think of the talk they have just heard?
6 Why does Peter want to contact Geoff?

Peter	Well, that was very interesting, didn't you think?
Geoff	Oh, definitely. Although I'm not sure that I agree with everything she said. The effect that e-commerce is going to have on jobs, for example. I really don't see that it will mean fewer personnel, at least not in the short term.
Peter	Oh, yes, I guess you are probably right there. But some of the other issues are things we have already come across. I wish I had heard about them a year ago – we could have saved ourselves a lot of problems when we first set up our Internet presence.
Geoff	I'm sure that's true. What kinds of things do you use the Internet for?
Peter	Well, at the moment we are mainly using it to provide information to our customers. They can find out about the services we offer, contact details, customer reviews, that kind of thing. But we are planning to make it more interactive, to put our core business on the website.
Geoff	What's your area?
Peter	Travel. Business travel. We're one of the largest business travel providers in the UK. We basically organize travel for other companies – mainly flights and hotels. How about you?

Geoff	I work for Western Credit Group – it's a small banking organization in the States. But my field is IT and my main concern at the moment is advising clients on the uses of the Internet and e-commerce.
Peter	Are you based here in London?
Geoff	Yes I am. Here's my card.
Peter	Thanks. Let me give you mine. Perhaps I can give you a call sometime. At the moment as I said, we are using our website to provide information, but our people also use it to book tickets and hotels for clients. So we are looking to develop our own capabilities in e-commerce.
Geoff	By all means, give me a call and we'll set something up.

12.11 *Roleplay – Networking*

Networking means making contact with other people who might be able to help you, or who might be useful contacts for you or your company. For many business people this is an important activity when attending conferences, seminars, receptions and similar functions.

A What do you normally do when you meet someone in the business world, for example at at conference or a reception? Tick the ones you would do in your own country. Then put a star next to the ones you think would be normal in an English-speaking country. Add your own ideas to the list.

- Give them your business card
- Introduce yourself
- Ask their name
- Ask who they work for
- Ask how much they earn
- Find out what field they work in
- Talk about something neutral
- Tell them what you think of the conference/the reception/the seminar
- Discuss the possibility of meeting
- Arrange a meeting

B Which of these did Geoff and Peter do? In what order?

C Here is some useful language to use when you first make contact with someone.

May I introduce myself? I'm ... from ...
Well, that was an interesting presentation, wasn't it?
What did you think of the last presentation?
Here's my card.
Do you have a business card?
I work for ... . I don't know if you have heard of us, we are in ...
Whereabouts are you based?
What field are you in?
What line of work are you in?
Perhaps we could meet up sometime. We might be able to use your services.

D Write a conversation between yourself and one of these people who you have just met.

ABC Online Training Systems **John Smith** *Managing Director*	Asia Tours **Dewi Sutanto** *Head of Marketing*	MRS Industrial Machinery **Noriko Kensuke** *Technical Sales Executive*

If possible, record the conversation. Then review your work and think about ways to improve it.

Lesson summary

Here are some of the things you practised in this lesson:

● Useful language for making and dealing with enquiries. (see **12.4**)
● Polite requests:

> *Could you tell me a little more about the services you offer?*
> *Please could you despatch the order as soon as possible as it is required urgently?*
> *I would be grateful if you could let us have your reply before the end of this week.*
> *Could you possibly send us some samples over this afternoon?* (see **12.7**)

● Offers:

> *Can I help you?*
> *I'll call him for you, if you like.*
> *Would you like us to send you over some catalogues and price lists?* (see **12.7**)

● Useful language to use when you first make contact with someone:

> *May I introduce myself? I'm ... from ...*
> *Well, that was an interesting presentation, wasn't it?*
> *What did you think of the last presentation?*
> *Here's my card.*
> *Do you have a business card?*
> *I work for ... . I don't know if you have heard of us, we are in ...*
> *Whereabouts are you based?*
> *What field are you in?*
> *What line of work are you in?*
> *Perhaps we could meet up sometime. We might be able to use your services.*

Suggestions for further practice

1 Make use of opportunities to meet people, at international trade fairs, business seminars and similar gatherings. If you cannot take part in these conversations, listen to other people introducing themselves.

2 Choose some of the exercises in **12.5**, **12.10** and **12.11** and do them again, using different contexts. Try to improve on your previous attempt. Think carefully about ways to improve your performance.

3 Look in a grammar reference book for more explanation and practice about polite requests, offers, introductions and ability.

4 Go through the conversations and exercises in this unit and look for words you are not familiar with. Try to find groups of words, for example make a list of all the words relating to ability and capability (*can, able to, ability, capable of, capacity for*). Record these groups of words in a vocabulary notebook and learn how to use them.

13 **THE ENERGY BUSINESS**

The two texts in this section concern one of the world's most important and valuable commodities. The first text provides basic information about the oil industry while the second deals with the search for alternative sources of energy.

In this unit you will:
◆ read about changes in the energy industry
◆ practise your reading skills
◆ develop your understanding of vocabulary: synonym and metaphor

Text 1: The Oil Business

13.1 *Warm-up questions*
● Which energy sources do you use in your home? In your place of work? Oil? Gas? Electricity? Nuclear power? Wind? The sea? Solar power?
● Which is the most important in your country?
● Which is the most expensive? How much is a litre of petrol in your country?

Reading

13.2 *Skimming and scanning*

Read the text on the next page to find answers to these questions.
1 What do the letters OPEC stand for?
2 Will we always need to use oil as a source of energy?

The Oil Business

What are the world's oil resources?

The world has about 1,000 billion barrels of proven crude oil reserves with the largest amounts to be found under Saudi Arabia, Iraq, United Arab Emirates, Kuwait and Iran in the Gulf. Venezuela has the next largest reserves, while in North America there are major deposits in all of Mexico, the US and Canada. Russia and China also have large proven reserves but, along with the 5 US, they are pumping at rates which will cease to be sustainable far sooner than their Middle East counterparts. In Central Asia, Kazakhstan has large oil reserves which have not been fully exploited to date. Africa has significant deposits in Libya, Nigeria and Algeria, while large North Sea deposits are exploited mainly by Norway. 10

Are we running out of oil?

Oil is a finite resource which could eventually run out. World consumption today is about 70 million barrels a day and oil producers expect this to rise to 100 million barrels by 2020. The Organization of Petroleum Exporting Countries (OPEC) says its reserves are sufficient to last another 80 years at 15 the current rate of production. What is more likely is that there will always be oil around, it will just become harder to extract, of poorer quality and more expensive. That is why many energy companies are currently investing large sums to find alternative sources of energy to reduce the world's reliance on oil. 20

What is the significance of OPEC?

The 11 members of the OPEC produce about 40% of the world's crude oil. However, non-OPEC countries consume large amounts of the oil they produce, so about 60% of the oil traded internationally comes from OPEC countries. OPEC's share of world oil production has been much higher in the 25 past and is set to rise considerably in the coming decades, as member countries hold more than 75% of the world's proven oil reserves. This is partly the result of the tendency outside OPEC producers to pump oil at full capacity while members subscribe to a quota system to regulate market prices.

What causes fluctuations in oil price? 30

Events on the international stage can create a climate of uncertainty which can lead to rises in oil prices. More important – like any market – is the equation between how much oil is pumped by the producers and the demand for oil among consumers. Politics have also played a part in the past, as in 1973 when OPEC members – led by Saudi Arabia – cut the oil supply to punish the West 35 for supporting Israel in the Arab-Israeli war. The move caused oil to jump from $3 a barrel to $12, causing economic crises in the developed world which had come to rely on cheap energy. Since then, OPEC's share of the oil market has

dropped because more oilfields outside the organisation have come on
stream. For many years OPEC was also unsuccessful in getting members to 40
stick to their own quotas. Higher prices since March 1999 came about as
OPEC members agreed to cut their output – and stuck to quotas – to address
an oil glut caused by a drop in demand after the Asian financial crisis. The oil
cartel was joined by a number of other exporters, notably Mexico, Norway
and Oman, increasing the OPEC-plus group's share of world output to 56%. 45

Who benefits from high oil prices?

The current buoyancy of oil prices offers most to cash-strapped non-OPEC
countries like Russia. It is unrestricted by OPEC quotas yet reaps the rewards
of high prices created by OPEC. Having seen the cycle of oil boom and bust
over the years, OPEC itself now has "market stability" as its watchword. An 50
example of this ethos was seen in 1990 when Iraq invaded Kuwait, threatening
to send oil prices rocketing. Prices did rise amid the uncertainty, but OPEC
also agreed to raise quotas to replace the 3 million barrels per day removed
from the market. On the other hand, the spikes of 1973 and in the 1980s may
have brought prosperity, particularly in the Gulf oil sheikhdoms, but they also 55
reduced demand and disrupted investment in oil projects in the medium term.
Ironically, it tends to be non-OPEC countries which are hurt more by
extremely low oil prices. Ease of access and quality mean that Middle Eastern
oil, in particular, is the most profitable and cheapest to produce in the world.

Can the world wean itself off oil? 60

It will have to eventually, but oil is too important on too many levels for that
to happen soon. Experts say the world's energy future could lie in renewable
sources like wave, solar, hydro-electric and wind power, and fuel cells, which
release energy from hydro-carbons chemically rather than through
combustion. But while oil remains an available and relatively inexpensive 65
resource, it will no doubt remain the backbone of economic power and
political influence in the world.

[*Source: BBC Business News*, 24 March 2000]

13.3 *Vocabulary*

Choose the best meaning:

1 billion (*line 1*)

    a 1,000,000
    b 1,000,000,000
    c 1,000,000,000,000

2 sustainable (*line 6*)

    a able to increase
    b able to make a profit
    c able to continue

3 finite (*line 12*)   **a** fine
                               b limited
                               c final

4 alternative (*line 19*)   **a** opposite
                               b reverse
                               c other

5 is set to (*line 26*)   **a** has
                               b will
                               c established

6 come on stream (*line 39–40*) **a** started production
                               b failed
                               c started slowly

7 glut (*line 43*)   **a** disaster
                               b over-supply
                               c crash

8 cash-strapped (*line 47*)   **a** having too much cash
                               b short of cash
                               c having no cash

9 cartel (*line 44*)   **a** group of companies which work
                                  together, eg to fix prices
                               b group of companies which regularly
                                  meet together
                               c group of companies with same policies

10 wean (*line 60*)   **a** gently break the habit
                               b change
                               c become aware of

13.4 *Comprehension*

Read the text in **13.2** again.

1 What do the following numbers refer to?
   a 70 million barrels a day   **c** 11 members
   b 80 years   **d** 1990

2 With reference to the text, are the following statements true or false ?
   a Russia and China will probably exhaust their reserves of oil before
      the Gulf States do.
   b Finding oil in the future is likely to become harder.
   c OPEC is able to control the price of oil.
   d Politics is the main factor causing price fluctuations.
   e Non-OPEC countries are most affected by low oil prices.

3 The following paragraph is based on information found in the text. Fill in the missing words. Then check your answers by listening to the recording or looking in the **Answer key**.

> Oil can be found on all the continents of the world, the largest _____ being in the Gulf states. Although it is a _____ resource, OPEC believes it has enough for at least another 80 years. However, the oil companies are nonetheless investigating _____ sources of energy. OPEC is the key figure in the oil business and produces about _____ of the world's production – its share may well increase in the future. OPEC tends to favour a policy of _____ _____ and will increase supply if for any reason, e.g. _____, supplies to the world markets are reduced. While it continues to be a comparatively _____ source of energy it will continue to play a vital role in the political economy of the world.

4 Abbreviations: OPEC means the Organization of Petroleum Exporting Countries.

Do you recognize the following?

a NAFTA	**e** ASEAN
b WTO	**f** IMF
c EC	**g** PAC
d FTSE	

Text 2: Alternatives to Oil

13.5 *Pre-reading questions*

- Why are people searching for alternatives to oil as a source of fuel?
- What alternatives do you know?
- How important is nuclear power in your country?
- How much pollution is there in your capital city?

Reading

13.6 *Skimming and scanning*

Read the text on the next page to find answers to these questions.

1 How many serious nuclear accidents have there been?
2 What is the future for coal as a source of energy?

Alternatives to oil

by BBC News Online's Environment Correspondent Alex Kirby

The industrialized world stands aghast at the prospect of rising oil prices.
Paying more for oil means increases in the price of almost everything that
drives the rich economies. The possibility that oil prices could continue to rise
appals the Northern countries, who see no other way to fuel their growth. But
they have little room for manoeuvre, because they cannot determine the   5
prices. In the grip of a crisis, it is hard to argue that there may be a silver lining.
But the benefit of the present oil price hikes could be to focus attention on
the possibility of a world far less dependent on oil. Environmental groups have
for years been arguing that we shall all have to live radically different lives when
the oil reserves are finally exhausted. The truth is that they probably never will   10
be. Oil will simply become too expensive to compete with other fuels. Amory
Lovins, of the Rocky Mountain Institute, is fond of reminding audiences: "The
Stone Age didn't end because the stone ran out, and the Oil Age will be just
the same".

The Age of Coal   15

Before oil's supremacy, coal was king. It was the bedrock of the industrial
revolution in Europe and North America, and it still has a role to play. There
are enormous reserves of coal available, but it does give off large quantities of
the gases which are causing climate change, especially carbon dioxide (CO_2)
and sulphur dioxide (SO_2). Technology can help, up to a point, with   20
improvements like fluidized bed technology, which burns coal much more
efficiently and results in much less pollution. But it seems highly unlikely that
coal will ever recover its once-dominant position.

Nuclear puzzle

Some people still pin their hopes on nuclear power, which makes far less of a   25
contribution to global warming (though it is not entirely neutral). But in half a
century the world's nuclear industry has had at least three serious accidents.
Windscale (UK, 1957), Three Mile Island (US, 1979) and Chernobyl (USSR,
1986) are names etched into the global memory, synonyms for horrific
brushes with catastrophe. Many people therefore reject new nuclear plants in   30
the belief that more accidents are inevitable. And apart from that, the industry
still shows no sign of being able to get rid of its waste in safety.

Renewable fuels

A third category of fuel comes under the heading of renewables. Some are
tried and tested, like hydro-electric power, and many countries, for instance   35

Norway, are already exploiting them to the full. Wind and wave power have promise, as does biomass – crops like willow which grow quickly and are increasingly being used for fuel. Transport fuel based on renewable oilseed crops such as soybeans and rape seed also has potential. Solar power is coming on by leaps and bounds. There are already photo-voltaic cells which will 40
provide power on a cloudy British winter's day, or even by moonlight. They are expensive, but a lot cheaper than similar cells were a few years ago. For vehicles, many motor manufacturers believe the future lies in fuel cells, which will power cars as effectively as now, but without relying on oil. They foresee a change from an oil-based economy to one based on hydrogen. 45

Conservation

And there is what its supporters are fond of calling "the fifth fuel" – energy conservation. Most of us still waste fuel on a prodigious scale, and the savings we could make by greater efficiency, and by just switching off, are immense. The environment minister of an eastern European country told me in the early 50
1990s: "In the Soviet days, we did have thermostats in our homes and factories. When we got too hot, we just opened the windows".

Rising oil prices are the perfect excuse for second thoughts.

[*Source: BBC Business News*, 8 September 2000]

13.7 *Comprehension*

1 What do the following refer to?
  a (*line 17*)   it
  b (*line 31*)   apart from that
  c (*line 44*)   They

2 Are these statements true or false?
  a In the future oil will become the most expensive fuel.
  b Coal is a major cause of pollution in the world.
  c People do not like nuclear power because it is too expensive.
  d Hydrogen will be the main source of energy in the future.
  e A lot of energy is wasted.

3 What do you think? Will oil be replaced by other forms of energy?

Language focus

13.8 *Pronouns*

Pronouns (e.g. *some*, *they*) are the important words used by writers to connect together ideas in a text. A good reader must be able to understand what the pronouns refer to.

What do the following refer to?

1	(*line 5*) they	**5**	(*line 26*) it
2	(*line 10*) they	**6**	(*line 34*) Some
3	(*line 16*) It	**7**	(*line 44*) They
4	(*line 23*) its	**8**	(*line 52*) we

13.9 *Vocabulary*

A Synonyms

In line 29 the text refers to 'synonyms'. A good writer uses a wide range of vocabulary and tries to avoid repeating words by looking for *synonyms* (words with the same meaning). The words in the list **1–7** are from the text. Find a synonym from the list **a–g**.

1	aghast	**a**	predict
2	radically	**b**	enormous
3	exhausted	**c**	completely
4	neutral	**d**	worn out
5	exploiting	**e**	without effect
6	foresee	**f**	horrified
7	prodigious	**g**	taking advantage of

B Metaphors

When we use a word which belongs to one area, e.g. politics, in a different area, e.g. business, we are using a *metaphor*. For example, line 16, "...coal was *king*". The writer is using the word *king* metaphorically. Other examples are:

drives (*line 3*)	(as in motor vehicles)
bedrock (*line 16*)	(as in geology)
role to play (*line 17*)	(as in the theatre)
etched (*line 29*)	(as in drawing)

Practice

Look at these words again in the text. Choose the meaning closest to the text:

1 drives	**a**	moves forward
	b	turns
	c	rides through
2 bedrock	**a**	heart
	b	beginning
	c	foundation
3 has a role to play	**a**	is involved
	b	has a responsibility
	c	is playing
4 etched (into the global memory)	**a**	well remembered by everybody
	b	drawn from memory
	c	little known by most people

14 | CHECK YOUR PROGRESS

14.1 *Vocabulary*

Find one word that doesn't fit in each of these groups. Cross the word out.
Add two or three more words to each group.

Finance	Currencies	Companies	Energy
stock market	sterling	Microsoft	renewable
currency	baht	American Express	fluctuations
application form	rouble	British Airways	oil
interest rates	euro	FTSE 100	nuclear
shares	gold	Honda	reserves

14.2 *Telephone language – jumbled sentences*

Put these sentences in order to make a telephone conversation.

a Bye.
b Do you know when she'll be back?
c Good morning. Interactive Systems. How can I help you?
d I'd like to speak to Erika Stolle, please.
e I'm afraid she's not here today. Can I take a message?
f Okay, in that case I'll call again tomorrow.
g She should be here tomorrow.
h Thank you. Goodbye.

Correct order: ____ ____ ____ ____ ____ ____ ____ ____

14.3 *E-commerce and banking*

Fill in the missing words to complete this summary. Choose words from the box below.

Information technology has radically _____ many industries, especially banking. Banks can _____ more information, use _____ paper, and process transactions more _____ and more cheaply. As a result, customers can check their _____, pay bills and _____ money without ever _____ a bank.

---

accounts   changed   different   entering   immediately   less
money   much   pay   quickly   store   withdraw

14.4 *Idioms*

a After several years i_____ t_____ r_____ , Amazon.com finally became profitable in 2001.

b Sorry I didn't get back to you earlier – I was t_____ u_____ in a meeting.

c Plans to expand the company have been p_____ o_____ h_____ because of the recession.

d Can you call Xerox? The photocopier is o_____ t_____ b_____ again.

15 | MAKING ARRANGEMENTS

In this unit you will practise:
◆ making appointments and organizing times to meet
◆ making travel arrangements
◆ talking about requirements
◆ talking about schedules, plans and arrangements in the future

Language:
◆ future tenses and definite plans
◆ travel timetables

Introduction

15.1 *Travel arrangements*

● Do you enjoy travelling? Do you like flying? Why/Why not?
● Do you travel a lot in your job? Where to? How often?
● Who makes your travel arrangements for you? You yourself? Your secretary? The travel coordinator in your company?

Look at the letter on page 153 and the following e-mail and answer these questions:

1 Where is Ray Smith planning to travel to?
2 When does he have to be there?
3 What is the purpose of the trip?
4 Who is he meeting?
5 Where is he going to stay?

SUNRISE PRODUCTS PTE
Head Office: Jalan Gajah Mada 279
Kota, Jakarta Utara 37106
Telephone: +62 21 860 3700 fax: +62 21 866 3715
e-mail: ho@sunrise-products. co.id

Ray Smith
Head of Overseas Marketing
International Plastics
35–75 Greenhurst Place
Croydon
Surrey CR8 4EZ

6th April

Dear Ray

I have made the arrangements at this end for your visit to us. Our chairman can meet you on May 9th and we have set aside May 11th for negotiations between yourself and the key people here. So can you arrive the weekend of 6th–7th May? This would give me a chance to show you round our plants on Monday 8th May and answer questions you may have. Please let me know ASAP if these dates suit you.

I suggest you stay at the Hotel Borobodur Intercontinental. It is the closest to our offices. Let me know your time of arrival and I will arrange for a car to pick you up at the airport.

Hope to hear from you soon
Regards

David Sitorus

David Sitorus
Operations Manager

From: Ray Smith <rsmith@mda.com>
To: Kate Jones <kjones@mda.com>
Date: Wednesday 28th April
Subject: trip to Indonesia

Kate

Can you make all the arrangements for this trip for me. I would like to leave on the Thursday and arrive on Friday so that I have the weekend to recover and prepare! Any airline will do (within reason!), business class of course. Send the arrival times to David Sitorus as he offered to send a car to meet me at the airport. I'd like to get the return flight on Friday (12th May) if possible — if not, the next day would be okay but I need to be back in time for my son's birthday on Sunday 14th.

Can you organize the room bookings too? If possible go with the one they have suggested.

Thanks

Ray

15.2 *Vocabulary*

Match these expressions from the letter and e-mail message with their meanings:

1	will do	**a**	not late, before something starts
2	in time for	**b**	to rest (after a journey)
3	to recover	**c**	as soon as possible, urgently
4	go with	**d**	will be okay, will be acceptable
5	to pick up	**e**	to agree with, to use what someone has suggested
6	ASAP	**f**	to meet someone (in a car)
7	be back	**g**	return (home)
8	to show round	**h**	to organize a visit or a tour (of a factory, a house, a tourist attraction)

ଲ *Listening 1*

15.3 *A phone conversation*

Kate Jones is on the telephone to Janet Brown of BTL. She is organizing Ray Smith's business trip to Indonesia. Before you listen, look back at **15.1** and write down some of the things that Kate is going to ask for. When you listen, check whether your predictions were right.

Janet	Good morning, Business Travel Limited. Janet Brown speaking. How can I help you?
Kate	Oh, hello, this is Kate Jones from International Plastics. I want to arrange a trip to Indonesia for next week for my boss.
Janet	Right, is it to Jakarta?
Kate	Yes, leaving next Thursday if possible.
Janet	4th May?
Kate	Yes that's right.
Janet	Any preference as to airline?
Kate	Not really, as long as it is a good one.
Janet	Okay, well there is a Singapore Airlines flight via Singapore. That leaves at 9 pm and arrives at 11.30 pm the next day.
Kate	Gosh that's a long flight. Isn't there anything direct?
Janet	Don't forget there's a time difference of six hours between London and Indonesia. But anyway let me check what else is available. ... There is a KLM flight via Amsterdam. It leaves

	Gatwick at 7 am, arrives Amsterdam at 8 and the connecting flight leaves Amsterdam at 10. That would get you into Jakarta at 10.30 am on Friday.
Kate	So that is … 17 and a half hours. That's a bit better. I think 7 am is a bit early though, have you got anything else? Heathrow would be better than Gatwick.
Janet	Let me check, hold on a minute. Oh yes, Emirates, there is a flight at 12.30 midday on Thursdays, with a good connection in Dubai, then arriving in Jakarta at 13.10.
Kate	What is Emirates like, is it a good airline?
Janet	Oh, yes definitely. It won the Business Travel Magazine airline prize for two years running. It's very good.
Kate	Okay, that's fine. Can you check availability?
Janet	Of course. Business Class?
Kate	Yes.
Janet	When is the return?
Kate	The following Friday.
Janet	12th May. Okay. Oh, Emirates don't have any flights from Jakarta on Friday. There's a flight on Saturday morning, 8 am arriving back at Heathrow on Saturday evening at 8 pm. Or there is a flight on Thursday morning, same times.
Kate	I think Saturday would be better. Can you book that provisionally and I'll confirm it in an hour or two?
Janet	Certainly. Just one passenger?
Kate	Yes.
Janet	Can I have the name?
Kate	It's Ray Smith. How about the price?
Janet	Three thousand two hundred and seventeen pounds, including airport taxes.
Kate	One more thing, can you book the hotel in Jakarta. It's the Hotel Borobodur Intercontinental. Just a standard single room.
Janet	Fine. I'll book that for you. Will you ring back to confirm the booking after you have spoken to Mr Smith?
Kate	Yes, sure. Sorry, what is your name again?
Janet	Janet Brown. My direct line is 020 7844 3775.
Kate	Okay, I'll talk to you later. Thanks a lot.

15.4 *Listen for the details*

Listen to (or read) the telephone conversation again and fill in this booking form.

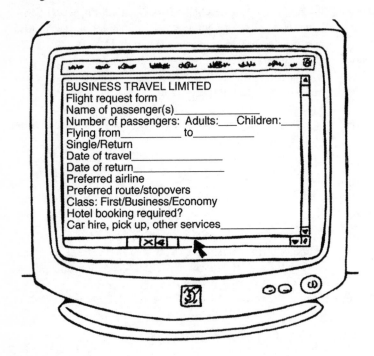

BUSINESS TRAVEL LIMITED
Flight request form
Name of passenger(s)_____
Number of passengers: Adults:___Children:___
Flying from_____ to_____
Single/Return
Date of travel_____
Date of return_____
Preferred airline
Preferred route/stopovers
Class: First/Business/Economy
Hotel booking required?
Car hire, pick up, other services_____

Writing

15.5 *Over to you*

Choose **A** or **B**

A Look back at the letter in **15.1**. Write a letter inviting a visitor from overseas to your company. Include relevant details about when to come, where to stay, what you have planned for your visitor.

B Look back at the e-mail in **15.1**. Write a similar e-mail to your secretary, or to the travel section in your company, asking them to organize a trip for you. Make sure you include all the relevant details.

When you have finished, check your work and try to improve it.

🎧 *Listening 2*

15.6 *Confirming travel arrangements*

Kate Jones has confirmed the travel arrangements with Ray Smith. Now she is talking to BTL again. Listen to (or read) the conversation and answer these questions.

1 What changes did Ray Smith make to the travel arrangements?
2 What was the problem with the hotel that Kate requested?
3 Where is Ray Smith going to stay?
4 How will he get the ticket?
   a He is going to pick it up at the airport.
   b Kate Jones will pick it up from BTL.
   c BTL will send it over by courier.
   d BTL will mail the ticket to Kate.

5 How will Kate pay for the ticket?
   a In cash   c Using a credit card, over the telephone
   b By cheque   d BTL will send a bill to be paid later.

Janet	Hello, Business Travel Limited. How can I help you?
Kate	Is that Janet Brown?
Janet	Yes.
Kate	Hi, it's Kate Jones from International Plastics. I talked to you about an hour ago about my boss's trip to Indonesia.
Janet	Yes, that's right. Hello Kate. Is everything okay?
Kate	I've spoken to Mr Smith and those flights are fine. Can you confirm them for us?
Janet	Sure, I'll do that right now. I'll fax you over a copy of the itinerary just to check all the details are correct. You have an account with us, don't you?
Kate	Yes, that's right.
Janet	So I can just invoice you for the tickets. I'll send the tickets out in the post tonight, unless you want them couriered over?
Kate	No the post should be fine, as long as they arrive by Monday at the latest. Did you manage to get the hotel booking?
Janet	Just let me check. ... Oh, there's an e-mail from our Jakarta office. *(reading)* "The Hotel Borobodur is completely full next week". There is an international conference of some sort. Our agent in Indonesia suggests the Hilton hotel. It's also very

nice and it's quite convenient for the airport and the business district.

Kate   Okay, I'm sure that will be fine. Can you just go ahead and book that?

Janet   Sure. What we can do is book the room, and charge you a booking fee. Then Mr Smith can pay the hotel bill directly. Is that okay?

Kate   That's fine.

Janet   Okay, I'll get a fax from the hotel confirming the booking and send that to you with the airline tickets.

Kate   Great. Thanks a lot. You've got our address for the tickets, haven't you?

Janet   Yes, we have. Who shall I address it to?

Kate   Can you mark it "For the Attention of Kate Jones or Ray Smith, Marketing Department"?

Janet   Sure. Anything else?

Kate   No I think that is all. Thanks a lot, Janet.

Janet   You are welcome. Bye.

Now complete this itinerary from BTL:

BUSINESS TRAVEL LIMITED
ITINERARY

Ticket for Mr Ray Smith

Thursday ____ May Depart London _____ Airport	Flight EMI 7721	____
Arrive Dubai International		21.45
Depart Dubai International	Flight EMI 2190	23.00
Friday 5th May Arrive Jakarta Soekarno-Hatta		_____
_____ 13th May Depart Jakarta Soekarno-Hatta	Flight EMI 2191	_____
Arrive Dubai International		14.05
Depart Dubai International	Flight EMI 7720	15.20
Arrive London _____ Airport		_____

Special meals: normal meals / vegetarian / vegan / other (please specify)

Hotel _____ International. 5th May – 13th May (___ nights).

Type of room: single / double / suite

Invoice to: _____ Account Number IP23Z

Tickets: courier / first class post / customer collects / pick up at airport

Language focus

🎧 15.7 *Talking about future plans*

There are several ways to talk about the future in English (see **Unit 9**). When you want to talk about definite plans and arrangements, especially travel plans, you normally use present tenses.

Use the **present progressive** to talk about travel arrangements.

I'm flying to Paris this afternoon.
I'm staying at the Intercontinental Hotel.
I'm meeting the finance director tomorrow morning.
What time are you meeting him?

Use the **present simple** tense to talk about scheduled flights and travel timetables.

The plane leaves at 10 am and arrives in Amsterdam at 10.45 local time.
What time does the train arrive in London?

Practice

A Answer these questions about Ray Smith's trip to Indonesia.

1 When is Ray Smith going to Indonesia?
2 Where does his plane leave from?
3 What time does it take off.
4 How many days is he staying there?
5 Which hotel is he staying in?
6 What is he doing on the Monday 8th May?
7 When is he meeting the chairman of Sunrise Products?
8 What day is he flying back to the UK?
9 What time does his flight arrive back in the UK?
10 Who is meeting him at the airport in Jakarta?

B Make up your own itinerary. Then imagine you are explaining your plans to your secretary. Write a note telling her your travel plans.

> *I'm going to .... next week. My plane leaves at ... from ....*

C Write a conversation between yourself and a colleague. One of you is going on a business trip. The other one is asking about the details of the trip.

Check what you have written and see if you can improve it. Check the tenses carefully.

🎧 *Listening 3*

15.8 *Arranging a meeting*

● Do you attend a lot of meetings in your job? Who with? Where?
● Who makes the arrangements for meetings? You yourself? Your secretary? Your manager or his/her personal assistant?

Sometimes it is difficult to arrange a meeting with several people involved. It's almost impossible to find a time when everyone is free.

Look at this e-mail, and Ray Smith's diary. Suggest a good time to meet. Then listen to the two conversations and find out when the meeting will be held.

From: Ray Smith <rsmith@mda.com>
To: Kate Jones <kjones@mda.com>
Date: Wednesday 28th April
Subject: Meeting re IT recruitment

Kate

Can you set up a meeting with Barry Donovan and Helen Thomas from Personnel for next week? We need to sort out the proposal to recruit more IT staff. Must be Tuesday or Wednesday as Monday is a bank holiday and I'm off to Indonesia on Thursday early morning.

You have my diary. Anytime we can fit it in would be fine with me. Shouldn't take more than 45 minutes.

Thanks

Ray

TUESDAY 3RD MAY		WEDNESDAY 4TH MAY	
9:00	Visit BRF factory	9.00	Dentist
10:00	10.30 video conference Jakarta office	10:00	
11:00		11:00	
12:00		12:00	
13:00	Lunch with Mike	13:00	
14:00	Meeting with architects	14:00	
15:00		15:00	
16:00		16:00	Export seminar 4-6
17:00	Meeting with finance director re. Indonesian partners	17:00	
18:00		18:00	
19:00	Dinner with Paul Davies	19:00	
20:00		20:00	Pack for Indonesian trip

15.9 Listening for details

A Now listen to Kate telephoning Helen Thomas and Barry Donovan and answer these questions:

1 What is the problem with Thursday?
2 What is Helen doing on Tuesday morning?
3 Why can't the meeting be held on Wednesday afternoon?
4 Where will Barry be on Tuesday?
5 What appointment will Barry have to rearrange?
6 Where will the meeting be held?

Helen	Hello.
Kate	Is that Helen Thomas?
Helen	Yes.
Kate	Oh, hello, this is Kate Jones, Ray Smith's secretary.
Helen	Oh yes, hello Kate.
Kate	Ray wants me to fix up a meeting with you and Barry Donovan next week. It's about recruitment of IT staff.
Helen	Okay, let me just check my diary. I'm free all day Thursday.
Kate	That's no good, I'm afraid. He's leaving for Jakarta on Thursday. It will have to be Tuesday or Wednesday.
Helen	Okay, can you suggest some times?
Kate	Tuesday between 11 and 1, or Tuesday afternoon between 3 and 5.
Helen	I can't make Tuesday morning, I'm afraid. We're interviewing for the post of technical director. I could do Tuesday afternoon from 4 to 5. Any idea how long the meeting will take?
Kate	Ray thought no more than 45 minutes.
Helen	Okay, so that's a possibility. Wednesday afternoon is no good. I have a meeting in Birmingham. Wednesday morning would be okay though, up until about 12. I'm catching the 12.40 train up to Birmingham.
Kate	Okay, let me talk to Barry and see if he can make it on Tuesday afternoon. Can I call you back in a few minutes?
Helen	Sure. I'll be here until 6 tonight.
Kate	Okay.

Kate	Hello, Barry?
Barry	Yes.
Kate	Kate here. I'm trying to fix a meeting with you, Helen Thomas and Ray. Are you free on Tuesday afternoon at 4?
Barry	Sorry, Kate, I'm not coming in on Tuesday. I'm taking the kids to France for the bank holiday weekend and I've got the day off on Tuesday too. I'll be back on Wednesday morning.
Kate	Could we meet around 10.30?

> **Barry** Errm. I'm supposed to be meeting a supplier at 10.45. They are demonstrating some new software we are thinking of buying. I'm free all of Wednesday afternoon. Couldn't we meet then?
>
> **Kate** I'm afraid not, Helen has to go to Birmingham.
>
> **Barry** Okay, well, I'll tell you what, I'll see the software people in the afternoon. How's that?
>
> **Kate** Thanks, Barry. 10.30 on Wednesday 3rd May. I think it will be in Ray's office.
>
> **Barry** Okay, see you on Wednesday then.
>
> **Kate** Sure. Have a great weekend if I don't see you before.

B Fill in the diary for **either** Barry **or** Helen.

TUESDAY 3RD MAY	WEDNESDAY 4TH MAY
9:00	9.00
10:00	10:00
11:00	11:00
12:00	12:00
13:00	13:00
14:00	14:00
15:00	15:00
16:00	16:00
17:00	17:00
18:00	18:00
19:00	19:00
20:00	20:00

C Match these words from the conversations above with their meanings in **a–h** below.

1 a day off, the day off   **a** a job
2 bank holiday   **b** a one-day holiday
3 fix (a meeting, an   **c** computer programs
   appointment)   **d** not busy, available
4 free   **e** public holiday
5 post   **f** somebody who sells goods or
6 software   services to another company
7 supplier   **g** the children, (my children)
8 the kids   **h** to arrange

Lesson summary

Here are some of the things you practised in this lesson:

● Useful language for negotiating arrangements:
     How about Thursday morning?
     Could you make it on Wednesday afternoon?
     I'm afraid I'm not coming in on Tuesday.
     I can't make it on Tuesday but I could manage Wednesday morning.

● Talking about plans and arrangements:
     We're interviewing on Wednesday morning.
     He's flying to India on Friday.
     What time are you leaving?
     Flight GA 332 leaves at 7.30 in the morning.

Suggestions for further practice

1 Go through the conversations and exercises in this unit and look for useful expressions for making arrangements. Write them in your vocabulary notebook and practise using them in conversations and e-mails.

2 Think of some questions to ask someone about the arrangements for a trip. It could be a business trip that you are going on. Write the questions you would ask the travel agent who has made the arrangements. Or it could be a trip your colleague or your boss is going to make. Write the questions you would ask them about their trip.

3 Look in the **Language Reference** section at the back of this book and/or in a grammar reference book for more explanation and practice about the future tenses.

4 Look at the dialogues in this unit. Write similar dialogues making arrangements in your own company. Then write letters and e-mails confirming the arrangements.

16 | MEETINGS

In this unit you will:

◆ practise the language of meetings
◆ discuss cross-cultural differences in business

Language:

◆ seeking and giving opinions
◆ expressing reservation and disagreement
◆ seeking clarification
◆ modal verbs

Introduction

16.1 *Going to meetings*

● Do you attend meetings at work? How often? How long do they usually last? Who attends the meetings?

● Many people complain that much time is wasted in meetings and they often achieve very little? Do you agree?

● What are the main purposes of the meetings you attend?

16.2 *Vocabulary*

B Match the following words (**1–7**) with explanations (**a–g**).

Example: 1e.

1 agenda
2 chairperson
3 minutes
4 apologies for absence
5 item

6 to chair a meeting
7 to circulate (the agenda)

a the person in charge of the meeting
b to send copies of a document (e.g. an agenda) to a group of people
c the written record of what was said or decided at the meeting
d to be in charge of a meeting
e the list of items to be discussed
f something you say or write to say sorry for not attending
g one of the topics on the agenda

B Choose words from the list **1–7** above to complete the sentences.

1 The secretary will _____ the _____ for the next meeting to all participants at least one week in advance.

2 If anyone would like to add to the list of _____ on the agenda, please notify the chairperson beforehand.

3 Please read through the _____ of the previous meeting. If you feel they are inaccurate in any way, please let me know.

4 Only eight will be attending the meeting. The representatives from New York cancelled and sent their _____ .

♪ *Listening 1*

16.3 *The meeting*

A Pre-listening exercise

Which of the following expressions would you expect to hear at a business meeting?

1 Could you put me through to Marcia Solanas?
2 I really can't agree.
3 Yes, that's right.
4 Thank you for your application.
5 Please find enclosed my CV.
6 Can I take a message?
7 How do you feel about this?
8 If I could just interrupt here?
9 Who's calling, please?
10 Thank you for pointing that out.
11 I understand your point but...

B Listen to Part One of the dialogue. What is the purpose of the meeting?
What questions would you ask if you were there?

THE MEETING

Senior members of the management of Chambers Hotel, Mexico City
are holding a meeting in the Manager's office. Present are the
following: Peter Mathers (General Manager), Maria Gonzalez (Head of
Personnel), Johann Elias (IT Manager), Julia Hammell (General
Manager's Secretary) and Pablo Martinez (Sales Director).

PART ONE

Peter	Good morning. Hi.
Maria	Hello, Peter. How are you?
Peter	Fine, thanks.
Johann	Morning, Peter
Julia	Good morning.
Pablo	Morning.
Peter	Help yourself to tea and coffee. Okay. I think we can start now. Did you get the agenda I circulated?
Johann	Yes.
Maria	Yes, thank you.
Peter	Atsushi Morita and Carl Reich send their apologies. Atsushi and Carl have a meeting with an important client, Tariq Al Said, that couldn't be re-arranged. I think some of you may know Mr Al Said. That meeting will be a real mixture of cultural backgrounds – Arab, German and Japanese. Anyway... you should also have received the minutes of the meeting last month.
Maria	There's one question I'd like to raise here, Peter.
Peter	Okay.
Maria	The new rates of overtime pay for staff. I thought we said they would come into effect on 1st October not 10th October.
Johann	That's what I thought too.
Peter	Mm...Yes, I think you're right. I think it's just a typing error. Okay, we'll change that. Thank you for pointing that out. Anything else? No.
	Okay. The first item on the agenda today is bringing forward the date for implementing the changes to our software.

Bookings for next month are low, as is usual for that time of year. So, it should be a relatively good time to make changes. We all know these changes will be disruptive but going with it next month might be the least disruptive time. I wanted all of us to talk this through together before making a final decision. What do you think?

Johann When would the changes actually start?

Peter In two weeks' time. At the beginning of the month.

Maria Er... That is soon.

Peter The sooner the better. The current system keeps crashing

C Listen to the rest of the discussion (Part Two). Why is Maria Gonzalez unhappy with Peter Mather's proposals?

PART TWO

Maria Well... I'm not exactly looking forward to it whenever it happens. Are we confident that it's going to work properly? The last time we went through installing updated software, it was a nightmare. Do you remember the chaos there was? Nobody knew what was happening or what to do because they didn't understand how to operate the new software. People were tearing their hair out.

Peter Oh. It wasn't that bad, Maria. In fact...

Johann Can I come in here? As you know I wasn't working here when the previous changes occurred so I can't comment on that experience. However, this time nearly all the work will be carried out over one weekend and we should experience, at worst, only some minor adjustments during the following few days.

Maria I hope you're right, Johann.

Johann Don't worry it'll be fine.

Maria Nothing personal, Johann. I've every confidence in you. It's just computers I don't trust... or rather they always seem to break down at crucial moments.

Peter Are we agreed that the changes can happen at the start of next month?

Johann Yes.

Maria	Okay.
Pablo	Yes, that's fine.
Peter	Now, the next item concerns Securicare Services. We have been using this company to provide security for about three months now. Reports about their effectiveness have generally been favourable. However, there have been complaints, including some from hotel guests, about some of their security people being rude and rather bossy.
Pablo	Yes, I've been in touch with Securicare already about this matter. Perhaps I could ring them again ...

D Here is a list of the points that Julia Hammell made beforehand. Which of these are actually mentioned in the meeting?

- Atsushi and Carl send their apologies
- minutes of last meeting
- agenda received?
- finish by 5pm
- new desks in offices
- the company logo
- last year's sales figures
- security firm
- new software
- date of next meeting

16.4 *Comprehension*

Julia Hammell was responsible for taking notes and writing the minutes. Listen to the extract again. She also attended another meeting the same day and has got confused about what exactly happened in each meeting. Correct any errors in her notes.

MINUTES OF THE MEETING date: 28 August

1 Present: Peter Mathers, Maria Gonzalez, Carl Reich, Johann Elias,
   Julia Hammell

   Apologies for absence: Atsushi Morita

2 Approval of the minutes of the last meeting.
   Problem with dates – change new pay rates to start on the 10th.

3 *Topic 1*: date for new computers.
   Discussion: concern expressed by MG. AT assured the meeting
   that problems would be minimal – about 2 weeks.
   Action to be taken: new computers installed.
   Person responsible: MG.
   Deadline: the end of the next month.

4 *Topic 2*: problems with cleaning staff.
   Discussion: complaints about timekeeping.
   Action to be taken: contact Securicare.
   Person responsible: AT.
   Deadline: immediately.

6 Agenda and date for next meeting: not mentioned.

Language focus

16.5 *The language of meetings*

A In meetings we have to give our opinion but also various other skills
are practised such as interrupting, asking others to give their opinion,
disagreeing, expressing reservations, seeking clarification. Match the skill
(**1–8**) and the language (**a–h**).

1 interrupting
2 asking others to give their opinion
3 agreeing
4 disagreeing
5 expressing reservations
6 seeking clarification
7 delaying answering
8 getting time to think

a Mmm....well, I need to think about that.

b Can I get back to you on that? I'll need to do some checking before I can give you a firm answer.

c Sorry, I didn't quite follow that. Could you go over that point again?

d I'm not so sure about that.

e I respect your view of course. But I see the situation differently ...

f Exactly. I think we are in agreement there.

g What's your opinion on that?

h Sorry to interrupt but ...

B Which expressions from the dialogue in **16.3** are used to express the following?

1 interrupting
2 asking others to give their opinion
3 agreeing
4 expressing reservations
5 seeking clarification

🎧 *Listening 2*

16.6 *Cross-cultural differences*

> **i** What differences are there in the way people behave in your country and in USA or in Britain? In the USA it is common for workers to use first names when speaking to their boss. Does this happen in your country? In Britain and the USA silence in conversation can make people feel uneasy. In Japan people are not so uncomfortable when sitting together in silence. In the Arab world people stand much closer together than in Europe or Japan.

Helen Wallenberg is a British businesswoman who travels extensively on behalf of her employer, Globalcar, an international car hire company. She discusses some of the cultural differences that she has noticed when meeting foreign business contacts.

A Pre-listening

In the interview she discusses the following countries: USA, Spain, Japan, Dubai. What cultural differences do you think she will mention?

B Listen to the interview.

What does she say about the USA, France, Japan, Dubai? Did you guess correctly?

Helen	I never travelled very much before I got this job. But not long after I joined the company, things really took off and I was asked to do a lot of the overseas promotions. So, for the past five years I've been going abroad about once every few months.
Interviewer	Where?
Helen	We have offices all over the globe.
Interviewer	Your company has a lot in the Arab world, I believe.
Helen	Yes. I've been to Dubai and Qatar several times. These are Muslim countries and of course one has to be aware of expectations concerning female clothing, namely that you have to dress modestly, and the rules about no alcohol. They, I suppose, are the obvious things. What you also have to realize is that business happens slowly. People there, as in Japan too, like to get to know you personally and feel confident about you as an individual before doing business.
Interviewer	What about Europe and the States?
Helen	Well, each country has its own special way of behaving. The French for example shake hands each time they meet whereas the British generally only do so when they are introduced for the first time. Having said that, I wonder if things are changing. People travel so much nowadays and maybe these differences in behaviour are decreasing. Perhaps more important are differences in attitude. For instance, in the States people can ask quite personal questions about you and your family and you're expected to use first names almost immediately you meet.

Language focus

16.7 *Modals*

These words express permission, necessity, advice and obligation: *may, can, could, must, should, might, have to.*

Are the following sentences true about your culture?

*You **must** always arrive at meetings exactly on time. Otherwise people may think you are unprofessional.*
*You **should** shake hands when meeting someone for the first time.*
It is polite to shake hands with everyone when you are leaving.
*You **might** invite an important client to your home for dinner with your family.*
*You **may** sometimes talk to clients about their family and friends.*

See **Language Reference** page 215.

Practice

What advice would you give to someone coming to your country for business? Write two things you should do and two things you should not do.

You should   **1**_____

                 2_____

You shouldn't   **1**_____

                 2_____

Lesson summary

In this unit you have:

- practised the language of meetings
- considered cross-cultural differences in business

Suggestions for further practice

1 If you know or work with people from other countries, ask them about cross-cultural differences. What did they think was unusual or different about your country? Are attitudes to work the same or different in their country?

2 If you are interested in advertising, you might enjoy doing the following research. Find an advertisement for a product (e.g. a particular car) in newspapers and magazines in your country and then compare it with an advertisement for the same product in the American or British newspapers (the print version or a version on the Internet). Are they the same advertisement? For example, in some countries the advertisers might emphasize the smart appearance of a car but in others the car's technical qualities might be emphasized.

17 | THE CHANGING JOB MARKET

In this unit you will:
- ◆ read about changes in employment practice
- ◆ learn what makes a good paragraph
- ◆ practise another technique for building up your vocabulary

In many countries the job market is changing. For example, low-skilled jobs, particularly in the manufacturing sector, are decreasing while jobs in the service industries, such as tourism and call centres, are increasing. This chapter will focus on two of ways in which employment has been changing: outsourcing and downsizing

---

Outsourcing

17.1 *Warm-up questions*

- Who does the cleaning in your company? Is the work done by company employees or a cleaning firm? Does your company employ temporary staff for secretarial, security and catering work?

- Which of the following phrases would you associate with 'temps' (an abbreviation for temporary workers) and which with permanent employees?

job security	cheap labour	salary scale
flexibility	efficiency	trade union
company loyalty	cost cutting	casual labour
low motivation	stress	

- Does your company or a company you know use call centres?

Did you know that when Americans telephone Microsoft for customer support they are likely to be talking to someone in a call centre in India? It is predicted that Indian call centres could be employing up to 200,000 people and earning $3.7 billion per year by 2008. (*Times Higher Education Supplement,* 23 March 2001). (Call centres are companies employing large numbers of people to deal with customer requests on the telephone. They are particularly popular with banking, insurance, retailing and transport services.)

You are going to read a newspaper article about "outsourcing". Outsourcing means that one company hires another company to carry out certain activities. The purpose of outsourcing is to cut costs and to use specialists who have the skills to carry out a particular task. Outsourcing is typically used in catering, office cleaning, security services and computing.

Does your company outsource any work? Before you read the article in **17.2**, think about the advantages and disadvantages of outsourcing from the employer's and the employee's viewpoints.

Reading 1

17.2 *Skimming and scanning*

1 Choose the best title for the article:
   a Can an outsider do an insider's job?
   b It makes financial sense to outsource non-essential services
   c Issues in employment.

2 Find one advantage and one disadvantage of outsourcing in the text.

Advantage	Disadvantage

Replacing full-time staff with temps can save money. But it might not make sense for British Airways to do it, warns Bill Saunders.

Rumours were circulating last week that after a less than rosy financial showing of late, British Airways is to contract out tiers of its administrative structure, getting rid of many permanent PAs and replacing them with external temps. Outsourcing, as this practice is known, has been a significant business strategy over the past 10 years for keeping down payrolls. But not everyone is convinced it is the best way to run a company. At its most extreme, the principle is very simple: decide which people are essential to an enterprise, and get rid of the rest. Administrative staff are supplied, sometimes in bulk, by outside agencies and are generally employed as temps or on short-term contracts. Virtually nobody directly employs cleaners, so why not tackle the basic tasks of office administration the same way?

Many sociologists have been unhappy about outsourcing, predicting a grey "age of anxiety" in which nobody really works for anybody. But studies have tended to show that short-term contract workers are less anxious than their fully employed peers. Temps acquire a broad range of skills and experience, while those who stay put may have limited opportunities for learning anything new. Much of it is a question of mindset, of course. Temps are used to flexible working, but the thought that any Friday they might be replaced by outsourced staff does not do much for fully employed workers' peace of mind.

But what of the employers? While nobody disputes that outsourcing can be a valuable strategy, some are beginning to move against the trend. "There is a time to outsource and a time to insource," says David Hagan, a director at M&G Investment Management. "It is a question of getting the balance right." In his case, one of the factors in the balance is communication. As investment managers strive to become more accountable to their clients, they must have support staff who understand the business. "Nothing must be lost in communication," says Hagan, arguing that this can best be achieved if individuals work permanently together.

Miranda Smyth, head of marketing at specialist legal recruiters ZMB, says that the need for good understanding makes outsourcing an entire operation very difficult. There are jobs that are best tackled by outsiders – strategic analysis, for example, which obviously benefits from a fresh set of eyes with no emotional attachment. But even apparently straightforward functions, such as typing, can be difficult for an outsider. All ZMB's documents conform to a house style, and unless the person entering it into the system understands it, the job will have to be done again. "The fact is that an employee using their knowledge of the structure and the politics of an organisation will get the end product signed off more quickly," says Smyth.

There are advantages for employees too. "Keeping staff in-house," says Hagan, "gives people a chance to develop themselves". Properly managed, the stability of a regular job can be as dynamic as the hurly-burly of the short-term contract. "People have the opportunity to work in several areas, and to test the waters in something which may not immediately appeal." The opportunity to develop new skills is, he says "the essence of a happy workforce". It goes without saying that well-trained and happy employees are more likely to "add value" beyond their basic job description.

As yet the trend towards outsourcing shows no sign of abating. Perhaps David Hagan and Miranda Smyth take a more independent view because they have both had varied careers themselves. She qualified as a solicitor, and he was a research physicist. One does not have to be a rocket scientist to see the sense in their arguments.

[*Source*: "Can an outsider do an insider's job?" by Bill Saunders, *Guardian*, 20 March 2000]

17.3 *Vocabulary*

The following words appear in the article in **17.2** above. Choose the best meaning:

1 tiers
    (*line 8*)
    a one third
    b levels
    c most of

2 less than rosy
    (*line 7*)
    a reasonably healthy
    b not very good
    c better than expected

3 keeping down
    (*line 14*)
    a keeping good records
    b increasing
    c stopping from rising too quickly

4 virtually nobody
    (*line 22*)
    a very few people
    b almost real
    c nobody at all

5 does not do much for
    (*line 39*)
    a has a negative effect
    b has positive effect
    c has no effect

6 getting the balance right
    (*line 48*)
    a reaching a compromise
    b getting the right outcome
    c saving money

7 signed off
    (*line 73*)
    a eliminated
    b written
    c finished

8 it goes without saying
    (*line 85*)
    a it is obvious
    b it is silent
    c it is secret

9 One does not have to be
    a rocket scientist
    (*line 95*)
    a it's impossible
    b it's not easy
    c it's not difficult

17.4 *Comprehension*

1 What do the following refer to in the article in **17.2**?

    (*line 4*)   it

    (*line 38*)   they

    (*line 43*)   some

2 What has been the main reason for the popularity of outsourcing?

3 Which type of employee feels less stressed? Temporary or full-time?

4 Are these true or false statements? In which paragraph did you find the answer?

    a British Airways is going to retrain many of its staff.

    b Outsourcing will create more stress among the workforce.

    c Typing should not be done by outsourced workers.

    d A contented worker needs to develop new skills.

5 Why do you think the author states in the heading that "it might not make sense" for British Airways to outsource?

17.5 *Understanding text organization*

If a text is well written, each paragraph should have a clear purpose. Paragraph one in the text introduces the topic. What are the purposes of the other five paragraphs? Choose from the following:

- to conclude
- to put the employer's viewpoint (twice)
- to provide the academic viewpoint
- to describe the advantages of outsourcing

paragraph 1:   *introduction*

paragraph 2: _____

paragraph 3: _____

paragraph 4: _____

paragraph 5: _____

paragraph 6: _____

17.6 *What do you think?*

Which would you prefer? To work as a full-time permanent employee or as a temporary outsourced employee? Why?

Downsizing

Downsizing is a term which is commonly used when organizations talk about the need to become more efficient and reduce costs. However, from an employee's viewpoint it simply means employing fewer people.

17.7 *Warm-up questions*

- Have there been any major changes in your company's organization recently?
- Have working practices changed?
- Is the labour force increasing or decreasing?
- Which of the following words do you associate with downsizing?

to promote	make redundant	payroll
lay off	salary	recession
lose	benefit	to fire
strike	to get the sack	growth
let go	commuter	to get the axe

⚆ *Reading 2*

17.8 *Skimming and scanning*

1 How many companies are named in the text?

2 Choose the best title for the text:

    a South Korea's top conglomerates present restructuring plans.

    b South Korean companies face big job losses.

    c All change in South Korea's business community.

South Korea's top 30 conglomerates submitted their restructuring plans to an emergency economic committee on Saturday, Yonhap news agency reported.

It said the various proposals put forward by the firms, which include Hyundai, Samsung and Daewoo, highlighted the downsizing of chairmen's secretariats and greater responsibility on the management.

5   Industry sources said Hyundai pledged gradually to close down its composite planning office and concentrate on four or five key businesses, including the automobile and heavy industries.

Samsung said it would not close its chairman's secretariat but transfer it to
10   another company that would take charge of management.

It also outlined plans to secure foreign capital through the Goldman Sachs fund
and to launch capital ventures with foreign car manufacturers such as Ford and
Volkswagen.

LG said it would transfer its chairman secretariat's function to a board of
15   directors and dispose of financially weak sectors of its business group.

Daewoo, also planning a gradual closure of the chairman's office, will make
public its complete restructuring blueprint next week.

SK said it would do away with its planning office from next year and have
group chairmen register as top executives of five selected subsidiary
20   companies.

These group chairmen will pump in extra money by selling their stocks in non-
mainstream subsidiaries, Yonhap reported.

[*Source: BBC Business News*, 14 February 1998]

17.9 *Vocabulary*

Look at the following words in their context. Choose the word or phrase
which has the closest meaning to the original:

1 conglomerates (*line 1*)   **a** a large multinational company
                                  b a large group of companies producing a
                                        variety of products
                                  c a variety of companies

2 restructuring (*line 1*)   **a** reorganization
                                  b review
                                  c resignation

3 highlighted (*line 4*)   **a** pictured
                                  b emphasized
                                  c viewed

4 secretariats (*line 4*)   **a** secretary
                                  b office staff
                                  c office furniture

5 pledged (*line 6*)   **a** promised
                                  b agreed
                                  c considered

6 take charge of (*line 10*) **a** attend to
                              b assume responsibility for
                              c give help to

7 make public   **a** make free
    (*line 16–17*)   **b** announce
                              c describe

8 blueprint (*line 17*) **a** document
                              b paper
                              c plan

9 subsidiary companies **a** additional companies
    (*line 19–20*)   **b** companies owned by a parent company
                              c supporting companies

10 stocks (*line 21*)   **a** shares
                              b raw materials
                              c goods

17.10 *Comprehension*

Read the article in **17.8** again.

A Complete the statements with the most appropriate ending:

1 South Korea's biggest commercial organizations agreed
  a to give greater responsibility to some managers.
  b to cut the number of associated companies.
  c to redesign the structure of their organisations.

2 Unlike other conglomerates, Samsung decided to
  a reduce the chairman's responsibilities.
  b put the manager's secretary into a new office.
  c give responsibility for the chairman's office to another organisation.

B Match the companies and the information provided in the text:

	Daewoo	Hyundai	Samsung	LG	SK	Ford	Volkswagen
1 downsizing secretariats	✓	✓	✓	✓	✓		
2 looking for foreign finance							
3 closing its planning office							
4 publicizing plans shortly							

17.11 *Building your vocabulary*

Another way of extending your range of vocabulary is to learn words not separately but in "family" groupings. You could also add examples of word partnerships (see **Unit 3**). Fill in the gaps in the table below, using a dictionary if necessary.

Noun(s)	Verb	Adjective	Word partnership
1 management/manager	to manage	managerial	managing director
2 _____	to compete	_____	competitive advantage
3 transfer	_____	_____	transfer funds
4 earnings	_____	earned	earned income
5 _____	_____	registered	
6 _____	to highlight	_____	

Suggestions for further practice

1 Are any English language newspapers published in your country? Do they have a business section? What are the most important issues affecting your country's economy at the moment?

2 Imagine you are going to meet a group of foreign business people who want to know about changes in the economy of your country during the past year. Prepare a short presentation. If possible, discuss your ideas with an English-speaking colleague at work.

3 As well as newspapers, radio and television, the Internet is a useful source of international business news. Try some of the sites in the **Useful Web Addresses** section on page 229.

18.1 *Vocabulary*

Fill in the gaps in this e-mail. You can use words from the box below.

```
From: Ray Smith <rsmith@mda.com>
To: David Sitorus <ho@sunrise-products.co.id>
Date: Thursday 29th April
Subject: trip to Indonesia

Dear David

I will be _____ in Jakarta at Soekarno-Hatta
Airport at 13.10 on Friday 5th May. I'm _____
with Emirates and my flight number is EMI 7721. Can you
confirm that someone will be able to _____ me up
at the airport? By the way, I will not be staying at
the Hotel Borobodur as it is completely _____. I
am booked into the Hilton Hotel.

We are also _____ you some sample materials and
some technical documents by courier. You should have
those by Monday midday at the latest. Please let me
_____ if they do not arrive. They _____
coming with Europe and Asia couriers and the reference
number is JAK37274A.

I look _____ to seeing you again next week. Let
me know if there is _____ you would _____
me to bring from London.

Regards

Ray Smith
```

full arriving know anything travel forward sending like
pick will are want flying

18.2 *Questions*

Ray Smith's secretary is talking to the Managing Director about Ray's travel plans. These are the answers to some questions about the travel arrangements. Write the missing questions.

MD	When is Ray leaving for Indonesia?
Kate	He's leaving on Thursday, at midday.
MD	Who _____?
Kate	Emirate Airlines.
MD	How much _____?
Kate	Three thousand two hundred and seventeen pounds.
MD	Gosh, that's a lot. _____?
Kate	He's staying at the Hilton Hotel.
MD	How long _____?
Kate	Eight days. He's leaving the following Saturday.
MD	Who _____?
Kate	He's meeting the Head of Overseas Marketing, David Sitorus, when he arrives, and he's meeting the Chairman of Sunrise Products on Tuesday 9th May.
MD	How long _____?
Kate	It's an eighteen-hour flight.
MD	Well, ask him to come and see me as soon as he gets back.

18.3 *What would you say?*

a You are telephoning a colleague. You need to arrange a time for a meeting. Tomorrow at 11 am would be a good time for you. Make a suggestion.

b You want to use the photocopier but you don't know how it works. Ask someone for help.

c You are visiting another company and you would like to make a phonecall. Ask the secretary for permission.

d Your computer printer is not working. There are several sheets of paper jammed inside it. Explain the problem to the technician (on the telephone).

e There is a telephone call for your colleague, but he is not at work today. Explain this to the caller and offer to take a message.

f Your colleague is on the phone. He suggests a time for a meeting (tomorrow at 11). This is okay for you, so tell him you agree.

18.4

Complete these sentences with appropriate words which appeared in **Units 15–17**.

1 Ray Smith is planning a business _____ to Indonesia next month.
2 He is _____ at the Hilton Hotel in Jakarta.
3 There is a _____ leaving London at 10.30 and arriving in Dubai at 13.45 local time.
4 Please can you _____ a meeting with the Head of the Personnel Department on Friday?
5 I can't come to a meeting tomorrow but I'm _____ all day on Friday.
6 Before we start the meeting, has everyone got a copy of the agenda and the _____ of the last meeting?
7 In Britain people usually _____ hands the first time they meet someone.
8 More than 2,000 people will be _____ redundant when Fujitsu closes it's plant next month.
9 Many companies are replacing _____ staff with temps.
10 IBM has announced plans to _____ the number of sales staff from 3,000 to 2,500.
11 In Britain and the USA it is important to arrive at meetings _____ time.
12 Women travelling to the Middle East know that they _____ to dress modestly.
13 I'm afraid I don't _____ with you on this point. In my opinion it is a mistake to outsource secretarial services.
14 What's the _____ of a business class ticket from London to Frankfurt, return?

18.5 *Self evaluation*

a Look back over the units you have studied in this coursebook. What areas of your English do you think have improved? Vocabulary? Grammar? Speaking? Listening? Reading? Pronunciation? Writing? Making telephone calls?
b If a colleague asked you for advice on learning English, what tips could you give him or her? What are the best strategies for learning and practising English in your experience?

c Which areas of English would you like to continue to improve?

d What resources could you use to continue learning?
   ● Buy another book
   ● Use the Internet
   ● Watch TV and films in English
   ● Read newspapers and magazines
   ● Practise writing dialogues, letters and e-mails
   ● Find friends to talk to in English
   ● Find a pen friend or keypal to correspond with
   ● Other suggestions:

Don't stop working on your English just because you have finished this book. Set some new goals for yourself for improving your English over the next few months. Then write an action plan of things you can do to achieve these goals.

Look at the section **Taking it Further** at the end of this book for more ideas about ways to study English.

ANSWER KEY

Unit 1: Companies

1.2

1 Benton International Powders Ltd. **2** IT/computing and travel. **3** Multimedia Solutions Incorporated. **4** Benton International Powders Ltd. **5** Business Travel Ltd.

1.3

Company name	*Business Travel Limited*	*Multimedia Solutions Incorporated*	*Benton International Powders Ltd.*
Main area of business	*Travel*	*Website design*	*Manufacture of powder paints*
Products / Services	*Travel services for businesses: flights, hotels, briefings, meetings*	*Design and management of websites and e-commerce*	*epoxy resin powder paint*
Customers	*Shell, House of Fraser, IBM (UK)*	*financial services insurance brokering and underwriting travel services, computer retailing, vehicle leasing*	*Manufacturers of metal shelving, lampshades, vehicle components, metal garden furniture*
Location: Head office Subsidiaries	*London USA: NY & LA, Europe*	*Guildford Birmingham, Dublin, Manchester, E'dburgh, Paris, Rome, Madrid*	*Birmingham Surrey and other plants (total 6)*
When did it start up?	*1979*	*1993*	*1979*
Number of employees	*270*	*200+*	*480*
Other information	*Profits £1.3 million last year. Founded 1989*		*Last year turnover exceeded £25 million profits £4.8 million*

1.4

2 Operation and management of the rail network. **3** Broadcasting and Internet. **4** Television production and broadcasting AND hotels and catering. **5** Banking. **6** Computer hardware manufacture. **7** Insurance. **8** Design of computer software. **9** Computer hardware manufacture. **10** Petroleum production. **11** Petroleum production. **12** Advertising. **13** Design of computer software. **14** Publishing. **15** Vehicle manufacture. **16** Food and soap manufacture. **17** Retailing foods and consumer products.

1.5

Suggested answers:

1 a factory	a plant	a production facility	
2 a warehouse	a distribution centre		
3 a subsidiary	an agency	a sister company	a franchise
4 the head office	a parent company	main office	
5 a department	a section	a division	a branch
6 a multinational	a conglomerate	a group of companies	

1.6

1 established; **2** groups; **3** employees; **4** subsidiary; **5** brands; **6** owns; **7** goods; **8** on; **9** areas; **10** chains; **11** electrical; **12** number; **13** profits; **14** office.

1.8

1 3. **2** The production division. **3** Birmingham, Leicester, Salford, Glasgow and South East London. **4** Research and Development. **5** Faversham, in Kent. **6** The development of new products, quality control, technical assistance to customers.

Unit 2: Jobs and introductions

2.2
1 e. **2** b. **3** c. **4** a. **5** f. **6** d.

2.3

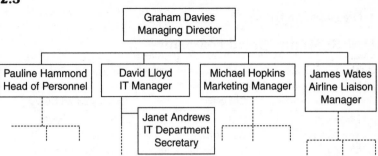

2.4

2 False. 3 True. 4 False. 5 True. 6 True. 7 False. 8 True. 9 False. 10 False.

2   **Pauline Hammond** is the Head of Personnel.

4 Jim Smith works for **the Los Angeles office of BTL**.

7 Michael Hopkins is going to have **lunch** with Jim Smith.

9 The Marketing Manager **introduced himself** to Jim.

10 Jim Smith is going to be working in London for about three **months**.

2.7

Speaker	Job	Speaker	Job
1	Personnel manager	2	E-commerce co-ordinator
3	Sales manager	4	PA to the Managing director
5	Receptionist	6	Accountant
7	Sales Representative	8	External Relations Director

2.9

1 He's the Head of the Finance Department.
2 She's an accountant with PriceWaterhouseCoopers.
3 He's from British Airways.
4 She works for the Sales Department of ICL.
5 They work for American Express in the traveller's cheque division.

2.10

1 Organizes; Authorizes.

Unit 3: Multinational companies

3.1

	Country	**Business activity**
Microsoft	USA	computer software
Volkswagen	Germany	automobiles
Unilever	UK & Netherlands	household products
Hitachi	Japan	electronic equipment
Barclays	UK	banking

3.2

1 Paragraph D. **2** 1917.

3.3

A new company: paragraph A.
Early growth: paragraph B.
Organization: paragraph C.
Product range: paragraph D.

3.4

1 b. **2** a. **3** b. **4** a. **5** c.

3.5

Different answers are possible. Suggested answers: merged; company; consumer; goods; brands; Holland

3.7

1 axe jobs. **2** raw materials. **3** logic. **4** dabbled in. **5** scuppered. **6** agribusiness. **7** a spending spree.

3.8

Year
1885   Lever Brothers founded.
1917   Lever diversifies into foods.
1930   Merger with margarine Unie.
1950s   Moved into chemicals, packaging.

1980s Got rid of packaging companies, most of agribusiness and speciality chemicals.

1984 Bought Brooke Bond tea brand.

1996 Niall Fitzgerald became chairman.

2000 Government action to end trading agreements.

3.9

1 Company newsletter. **2** business newspapers.

Reading 1 is from an official company history of Unilever. Reading 2 is from a BBC News report. Reading 2 is more critical of the company (*lines 25–40*) and uses more colourful expressions, e.g. "got rid of its packaging companies" (*line 32*), "spending spree" (*line 34*).

3.12

1 **a** (iv); **b** (ii); **c** (i); **d** (iii).

2 **a** General Motors; **b** General Electric; **c** Citigroup; **d** General Electric; **e** Wal-Mart.

3 Four.

4 Yes, IBM.

5 Automobiles.

6a two; UK; $51,632m; market value.

Unit 4: Job hunting

4.2

A **1** Bilingual Executive Assistant   **4** Head of Marketing

    2 Accountancy Clerk   **5** Sales Executives

    3 Exectuve Trainees   **6** Software Support Manager

4.3

a 6. **b** 1. **c** 1, 2. **d** 4. **e** 3. **f** 2. **g** 1, 2, 6 (3, 4, 5). **h** 3. **i** 2. **j** 5. **k** 1, 2, 6.

4.4

a Patrick Kiely: Job 1. **b** Teresa Soliz: Job 1. **c** Miriam Jax: Job 4. **d** Michel Delain: Job 2. **e** David Delgado: Job 6.

4.6

1 Miriam. **2** Patrick. **3** David. **4** Miriam. **5** Teresa. **6** Michel.

a Use simple past tense ("I worked ...") when talking about a period of time that is over (for example a previous job).

b Use present perfect tense ("I have worked …" or "I have been working …")
when talking about something that started in the past but is still continuing now,
for example the job you are doing at the moment.

4.7

decided /id/; worked /t/; started /id/; finished /d/; ended /id/.

4.8

1   Patrick is feeling unhappy. Roberto notices he looks "down in the dumps".
2   Patrick's job application was unsuccessful. (c)
3   He is going to apply for the job of Bilingual Executive Assistant.

4.9

1 False. **2** True. **3** False. **4** False. **5** True. **6** False. **7** False.

4.10

1 c. **2** f. **3** d. **4** e. **5** a. **6** d.

4.11

1   Top right hand corner of the letter.
2   At the bottom.
3   Top left, below your own address.
4   "Dear Sir", "Dear Madam", "Dear Sir or Madam" at the beginning.
    "Yours faithfully" at the end.

4.12

He's leaving for London on Tuesday but he hasn't sorted out all the arrangements;
the e-mail system is giving trouble; he doesn't know how to use it properly.

4.13

1 False. **2** True. **3** False. **4** True. **5** True. **6** True. **7** False. **8** True.

1 Pierre is **not** going to have a drink with Silvia.
3 Pierre's **doesn't have a secretary**.
7 Pierre's last assistant worked for him for **only 3 weeks.**

4.14

A **1** e. **2** d. **3** b. **4** a. **5** c.

B Suggested answers:
To Mike: Why don't you ask the travel section to take care of them for you?
To Alicia: I think you should look for another one.
To Alexandra: If I were you, I'd complain to personnel.
To Paul: Have you tried calling IT support?
To Julie: You shouldn't buy so many new clothes.

Unit 5: Letters and CVs

5.2

Appropriate: **a, c, f, h, i, k**.
Not appropriate: **b, d, e, g, j, l**.

5.3

1 In South Ealing, in London.
2 Web Designer with West London College of Higher Education.
3 Degree in IT with Business Studies (and courses in graphic design and usability design).
4 E-commerce consultant.
5 17 May.
6 Personnel Manager.
7 Multimedia Solutions Incorporated.
8 Yes – suitable qualifications and experience.
9 Yes, it seems quite effective but see the ideas in the rest of Unit 5.

5.4

Do's: **2, 3, 4, 5, 6, 7, 9, 11, 13, 15, 16**.
Don'ts: **1, 8, 10, 12, 14**.

5.5

1 Not mentioned.
2 None mentioned.
3 None mentioned.
4 Financial consultancy and planning advice on pentions, life assurance, savings, etc.
5 Yes – "long term prospects".
6 Not stated (probably yes).
7 Yes, although nothing specifically mentioned.
8 Probably – "posts throughout our European network".
9 Not stated. Almost certainly not.
10 Products and services only.
11 50–100.
12 Yes.

5.8

1 In Madrid.
2 Three.
3 St Joseph's College.
4 No information.
5 No information.

6 No information.

7 Yes.

8 Calle Prim 19, 4th Floor, 28004 Madrid.

9 National Gallery of Ireland, Comlink Computers.

10 Spanish, Maths, Economics, Physics, English and Art.

11 Spanish.

12 Advising customers and small businesses on their IT requirements. Sales, delivery and installation of PCs. Answering technical queries and dealing with IT problems.

13 The latest.

Unit 6: A job interview

6.2

1 Wanted to travel and work abroad, and also wanted to join his partner in Spain.

2 Working hard on his Spanish. Taking some other courses. Applying for jobs.

3 Feels fairly settled in Spain at the moment.

6.3

1 True. **2** False. **3** False. **4** True. **5** True. **6** False.

2 His girlfriend is Spanish.

3 He has had a number of job interviews.

5 Not completely clear – he has been working on his Spanish and has done some other courses.

6 He left the Bank of Ireland because he wanted to work abroad and his girlfriend was offered a job in Madrid.

6.4

1 decided. **2** felt. **3** have you been doing. **4** said / have been working. **5** I have been applying. **6** I've had / have turned down.

6.6

1 True. **2** False. **3** True. **4** False. **5** True.

6.7

1 **a** for/with. **b** in. **c** on. **d** down. **e** for. **f** back. **g – h** about.

2 **a** for. **b** about/in. **c** from. **d** on. **e** at/together.

3 **a** to turn down. **b** different from. **c** to take on. **d** to look at.

6.9

1 Five. **2** Patrick. **3** Teresa. **4** More relaxed? Patrick. More ambitious? Teresa. Had better Spanish? Teresa. Better English? Patrick. Was better qualified? Neither. They were both well qualified for the job.

6.10

1 d. 2 a. 3 b. 4 c.

Unit 7: Check your progress

7.1

1 Companies: multinational, firm
2 Job titles: Managing Director, Accountant
3 Job hunting: application form, advertisement
4 Describing people: ambitious, punctual

7.2

1 subsidiary. 2 established. 3 manages. 4 deals with. 5 like. 6 involved. 7 including. 8 merged. 9 how. 10 information. 11 for. 12 ran. 13 forward. 14 CV. 15 did. 16 offered. 17 seemed.

7.3

Listen to Part Two of the recording for suggested answers.

7.4

1 f. 2 d. 3 g. 4 e. 5 a. 6 b. 7 c.

Unit 8: Finance

8.1

Bill Gates has approximately $58.7 billion. The Nikkei, FTSE 100 and Wall Street are connected with stock markets.
1 stock markets. 2 unemployment. 3 interest rates.

8.3

Country	Currency	Price of a Hamburger Local currency	Dollars
Japan	Yen	Y294	2.78
European Union	Euro	€2.56	2.37
Brazil	Real	Real 2.95	1.65
Russia	Rouble	R39.50	1.39
United Kingdom	Sterling	£1.90	3.00
China	Yuan	Y 9.90	1.20
USA	Dollar	$2.51	2.51
Taiwan	New Dollar	NT $70.00	2.29
Indonesia	Rupiah	Rp 14,500	1.83
[Source: *Economist*, 27 April 2000]			

8.4

a 0.5 cents. **b** 6. **c** 12. **d** 3 per cent. **e** 2 per cent. **f** 2.5 per cent. **g** 1,000. **h** 500.
i rapid. **j** 5,000. **k** 1½. **l** one.

8.5

1 three point five per cent.
2 twenty two thousand.
3 ten point five.
4 two dollars seventy eight cents.
5 two hundred and ninety four yen.
6 one pound ninety.
7 nine million seven hundred and eighty four thousand five hundred and ninety six.
8 five million four hundred and eighty three thousand four hundred and ninety five.

8.6

1 exceeded. 2 flagship. 3 launched. 4 light-hearted. 5 converts. 6 expensive. 7 data.
a False. **b** True. **c** Yes according to the index.

8.7

A   1 harder, hardest
       2 dearer, dearest
       3 more efficient, most efficient
       4 better, best (*irregular*)
       5 luckier, luckiest
       6 more ambitious, most ambitious
       7 more interesting, most interesting
       8 more expensive, most expensive
       9 cheaper, cheapest
      10 costlier, costliest

B   1 biggest, best, more happy, more satisfied
       2 longer, largest, younger

8.8

1 A city trader.
2 Some did not believe it . Others soon realized there had been a mistake.

8.9

1b. 2a. 3b. 4a. 5a. 6a. 7c. 8b. 9b. 10a.

8.10

a True. b False. c False. d False. e False. f True.

8.11

1d. 2c. 3b. 4a.

Unit 9: Using the telephone

9.2

Christos can't speak to Jim Smith because Jim's line is busy – he is talking to someone else on the telephone already.

9.3

2 His phone number is 85983 *not* 85993.
3 His company's name is Multimedia Solutions Incorporated *not* Corporation.
4 He will be in his office this morning *not* this afternoon (He will be out all afternoon).
5 He wanted to be called back.

9.4

1c. 2a. 3a. 4a.

9.5

a five five nine nine zero nine two one
b seven eight four six two two five four
c eight five nine three zero nine zero zero
d zero four six six eight seven seven seven
e eight five seven four zero zero two one
f three three six four zero nine eight six

9.7

	Message 1	**Message 2**	**Message 3**	**Message 4**
Name	Racquel Boutier	*Liam Dwyer*	Paul Delgado	*Yasuko Kitamura*
Date	4th May	6th May	7th May	8th May
Dept./Company	*Anglo-Spanish Travel Services*	marketing department	SP Computers	Japan Tech Ltd
Tel no.	00 34 93 345 6488	extension 2931	094 3345 9704 extension 896	020 743526

Message 1

Hello, Mr Smith. This is Racquel Boutier. That's B-O-U-T-I-E-R . I work for a company called Anglo-Spanish Travel Services. I don't know if you are aware, but we are your agents in Spain. Liam Dwyer from your marketing department told me that you might be able to give us some ideas about the companies you used for your website. I must say, your site looks really impressive. Do you think I could come and meet you for about an hour? I am coming to London next weekend and I could come in any time on Friday afternoon, Monday or Tuesday morning. Could you let me know if that that would be convenient? My phone number is 00 34 93 345 6488. My email address is Racquel.Boutier@ASDS.com

This message was left at 12.15 on Monday, 4 May

Message 2

Hi, Jim, this is Liam Dwyer from the marketing department. I'm trying to set up a meeting for next week about the new website and I want to know when you can make it. Can you let me know whether Wednesday late morning or Thursday afternoon anytime would be possible? You can call me back on extension 2931.

This message was left at 10.50 am on Wednesday, 6 May

Message 3

Hello, I am Paul Delgado from SP computers. You left a message saying you wanted to speak to Pierre Blisset. Unfortunately Pierre is on vacation at the moment. Perhaps I could help. You can call me on 094 3345 9704 extension 896. My name is Delgado, spelt D-E-L-G-A-D-O. Thank you.

This message was left at 11 am on Thursday, 7 May

Message 4

My name is Yasuko Kitamura. I am the Deputy Sales Manager at Japan Tech Ltd. Could you please ring me on 020 743526? Thank you.

This message was left at 11.15 on Friday, 8 May

9.8

1f. 2d. 3e. 4c. 5g. 6a. 7b.

9.10

b A delay

9.11

1 False. 2 True. 3 False. 4 True. 5 True. 6 False. 7 False.

9.12

PA	Multimedia Solutions Incorporated, Development Section, good morning.
Jim	Oh hello, I'd **like** to speak to Christos Georgiou.
PA	He's on the other line at the moment. I'm his PA. Can I ask who's **calling**?
Jim	Yes, **this** is Jim Smith from Business Travel Limited. I'm **returning** his call from this morning.
PA	Oh yes, Mr Smith. **Hold** on just a second, I think he's just finished.
Christos	Hello Jim, sorry to **keep** you waiting.
Jim	No problem. What's up?
Christos	**It's** about the new version of your website. We had some problems with the changes you asked for last week, but it's all **sorted** out now. However, we are behind schedule and we are not **going** to be able to deliver next week.
Jim	Well, when do you think you will **be** able to deliver?
Christos	We only need two extra days. It'll be **ready** for installation by Tuesday of the week after next.
Jim	As long as we get it on the Tuesday there should be no problem. Are you sure there **won't** be any more delays?
Christos	Yes, I'm sure.
Jim	Okay, that's fine. But if anything else does come up, please let me **know** as early as possible.
Christos	Of course. If we have any more problems, **I'll** let you know immediately.
Jim	Thanks a lot. I'll give you a **call** at the end of next week anyway.
Christos	Fine. **I'll** speak to you then. Have a good weekend.
Jim	Bye.

9.13

a 2, 3. **b** 1, 4. **c** 4. **d** 4. **e** 3.

1c. **2**d. **3**b. **4**a.

9.14

1b. **2**c. **3**a. **4**a. **5**c.

9.15

Listen to the recording for suggested answers.

Unit 10: E-commerce

10.1

software	computing program, e.g. Word, Excel
hardware	physical components of computing, e.g. disks
PC	personal computer
telemarketing	selling via the telephone
e-commerce	electronic business, e.g. via the Web
network	system of interconnected PCs
search engine	program which searches through a database

10.2

1 search engine.
2 hardware.
3 the network.
4 software.

10.3

A It has caused great changes.
B1 100 times cheaper.
B2 Advantages: reduce paper records, store vast amounts of information, speed up the process of handling information, data can be more easily sorted and accessed, easier and faster communication between business people, customer can have access to information previously not so easily available, greater cost efficiency.
Disadvantages: fewer bank branches and fewer employees to deal with customers.

10.4

A 1e. 2c. 3a. 4b. 5d.

B 1 paper records.
2 information technology.
3 radical changes.
4 service industries.
5 essential information.

10.5

B im'portant, 'clever, ad'vertisement, 'total, a'fford, 'borrow, 'easy, ex'change, in'crease, 'special, ad'vise

10.6

1 E-zines. The message is targeted at a specific audience.
2 classified ads.
3 banner ads.

10.7

B Introduction 1 is probably better because the speaker introduces himself to the audience, and gives a clear description of content of his presentation. However, it is formal and less friendly than Introduction 2.

C 1 Introduce yourself, the purpose of the presentation and how things will be organized. Memorize the first few words.
   2 Signal each of the points.
   3 Brief summary, thank the audience and answer questions.

10.8

1, 4, 6 = concluding.
2 = starting a new point.
3 = introductions.
4, 5 = referring to a previous point.

Unit 11: Socializing

11.1

1 Dialogue 2.
2 Dialogue 1.
3 Dialogue 1: How about meeting; That would be great.
  Dialogue 2: We were wondering if ...; It's good of you to offer.

11.4

1 Julio da Silva.
2 Mr Smith.
3 Mexico City.
4 His card.
5 To buy him a drink.

11.5

A Several answers are possible. Here are some suggestions.

a How was your weekend ?
  Did you watch the football yesterday?
b How about getting together for a drink one night this week?
  Have you played much lately?
  We must have a game sometime.
c That's very kind of you
d Hello, Peter. How are things in the IT section?

e Excuse me. Are you Mr Andrews ? I'm ... from MS Development.
   Was the journey alright?
   Did you have a pleasant flight?
   Great weather we are having at the moment.
   I'm afraid the weather hasn't been very good recently.
B **a** 1. **b** 3. **c** 4. **d** 5. **e** 6.

11.6

1f. **2**d. **3**i. **4**h. **5**g. **6**c. **7**a. **8**e. **9**b.

1 got the green light.
2 red tape.
3 put on hold.
4 in the pipeline.
5 on the blink.
6 started the ball rolling.
7 tied up all day.
8 in the red.
9 a long shot.

11.7

A curry: India.
   paté: France.
   spaghetti bolognaise: Italy.
   borscht: Russia.
   taco: Mexico.
   couscous: Tunisia.
   sushi: Japan.

B **1** curry. **2** spaghetti bolognaise.

11.8

What would you like to drink?   A pint of Guinness, please.
What kind of wine would you like?   A dry white wine, please.
This is on me/It's my round.   Thank you very much.
Cheers!   Cheers!
Another one before you go?   I'd better not. I'm driving. Thanks all the same.

11.9

A *Suggested answer*: Thanks very much for offering. But really I just can't drink
any more. I have an important meeting early tomorrow morning.
B Oh, how interesting!

C

Asking questions politely	Answer: Yes	Answer: No
1 Excuse me, could you...?	Certainly.	
2 Is it all right to...?		Sorry. I'm afraid ...
3 Do you mind if ...?	Please do.	
4 Sorry to disturb you. Can I ...?	Yes, of course.	
5 Could I have a ..., please?	Here you are.	
6 May I ...?	Yes.	
7 Would you like some coffee?	That would be lovely. Thank you.	
8 Could you tell me... please?		Sorry.

a Would you like to put your coat there?
b Can I offer you a cup of coffee?
c How do you spell your name, please?
d What company are you from, please?
e Can I help you?
f Is it all right to smoke a cigarette in here? / Could you tell me where the smoking area is, please?

11.10

B **1** The first version is more polite.
   2 The second version is more polite.
   3 The first version is more polite.

Unit 12: Making contact

12.2

1 Business Travel Limited
2 He is trying to find out what sort of support he can get from specialized companies to expand the capabilities of his company's website.
3 His business card and some brochures.
4 **a** Probably not.
   b Yes, probably.
   c Probably not.
   d Yes, probably.

12.3

1 False.
2 True.
3 True.
4 False. Mike gave Jim his business card and a brochure about *his* company.
5 False. Mike Saunders' company has already set up interactive sites with full e-commerce capability for a number of clients.

6 True.

7 False. Mike suggested that Jim should look at some websites designed by *his* company.

12.6

Recep	Project Personnel, good morning.
Mike	Oh good morning, I want to talk to someone about getting some IT consultants in, on a temporary basis.
Recep	I'll put you **through** to our IT department. Hold on a minute.
Celia	IT recruitment. Celia Robins **speaking**.
Mike	Oh, good morning. My name is Mike Saunders, I work with a company called Multimedia Solutions. I don't think we have used your agency before.
Celia	How can I **help** you Mr Saunders?
Mike	We need to recruit extra web designers for a new contract. The project will probably **take/last** about one and a half to two months.
Celia	Right. How **many** people are we talking about exactly?
Mike	Five. We need people with **experience** in e-commerce, using Dreamweaver and Oracle database. Do you have anyone like that?
Celia	Yes, that should be no problem. When do you **need** them for?
Mike	As soon as **possible**. Say next week? I know that is short notice but we need to get them in pretty urgently.
Celia	Okay. We do have some suitable people, I need to check if they are **available** starting next week. I could fax or email some CVs over to you this afternoon.
Mike	That would be great. Can you give me some **idea** about cost?
Celia	If you need people for more than a month, around £50 an hour.
Mike	Right. Well if you have **suitable** people that would be fine.
Celia	Okay, well **leave** it with me and as I say I should be able to send you the details this afternoon.
Mike	Okay, I'll **give** you my email. It's M dot Saunders S-A-U-N-D-E-R-S at M-S-I dot co dot U-K. And the phone number is 020 7648 6868.
Celia	Fine. I'll be in **touch** this afternoon.

12.7

1a. 2c. 3b. 4d. 5e. 6f.

12.8

1 able to/can do.

2 capable of/can be/up to.

3 experience of/have already.

4 be possible/can guarantee.

12.10

1 Business Travel Limited.
2 Organizing travel – flights, hotels, etc. for other companies.
3 The Western Credit Group.
4 IT advisor.
5 Interesting, although they didn't agree with everything the speaker said.
6 It isn't clearly stated but probably to get some information and advice on setting up e-commerce.

12.11

A *This is what you might normally do when you meet someone at a conference or a reception in an English-speaking country, but of course there are different possibilitie*s:

1 Tell them what you think of the conference/the reception/the seminar *or* Talk about something neutral.
2 Introduce yourself.
3 Find out what field they work in.
4 Ask who they work for.
5 Discuss the possibility of meeting.
6 Arrange a meeting.

B 1 They talked about what they thought of the talk.
   2 Geoff asked Peter what field he worked in.
   3 Peter answered then he asked Geoff the same.
     Geoff gave the name of his company and explained about his job.
   5 Geoff gave Peter his card.
   6 Peter gave Geoff his card and suggested a meeting.
   7 Geoff agreed.

Unit 13: The energy business

13.2

1 Organization of Petroleum Exporting Countries.
2 No. There are alternatives available but it is likely to be a long time before it is replaced as the most important source of energy.

13.3

1b. 2c. 3b. 4c. 5b. 6a. 7b. 8b. 9a. 10a.

13.4

1 **a** World's daily consumption of oil.
  b OPEC's oil reserves are sufficient to last for 80 years.

   c The 11 members of OPEC.

   d OPEC increased production of oil in order to prevent prices rocketing and causing instability in the world economy.

2 a True. **b** True. **c** False – but it does have a very strong influence. **d** False. **e** True.

3 Oil can be found on all the continents of the world, the largest **deposits** being in the Gulf states. Although it is a **limited** resource, OPEC at least believes it has enough for at least another 80 years. However, the oil companies are nonetheless investigating **alternative** sources of energy. OPEC is the key figure in the oil business and produces about **half** of the world's production – its share may well increase in the future. OPEC tends to favour a policy of **market stability** and will increase supply if for any reason, e.g. **war**, supplies to the world markets are reduced. While it continues to be a comparatively **cheap** source of energy it will continue to play a vital role in the political economy of the world.

4 a North Atlantic Free Trade Area. **b** World Trade Organization. **c** European Community. **d** Financial Times Stock Exchange. **e** Association of South East Asian Nations. **f** International Monetary Fund. **g** Pan African Congress.

13.6

1 Three.

2 It will never recover its once-dominant position.

13.7

1 a Coal. **b** The belief that more accidents are inevitable. **c** Motor manufactuers.

2 a Probably true. **b** True. **c** False. **d** False. **e** True.

13.8

1 the Northern countries.

2 oil reserves.

3 coal.

4 coal's.

5 nuclear power.

6 renewable fuels.

7 motor manufacturers.

8 people living in the an eastern European county during the Soviet era.

13.9

A 1f. 2c. 3d. 4e. 5g. 6a. 7b.

B 1a. 2c. 3a. 4a.

Unit 14: Check your progress

14.1

Finance: application form. Currencies: gold. Companies: FTSE100. Energy: fluctuations.

14.2

c, d, e, b, g, f, h, a.

14.3

Information technology has radically **changed** many industries, especially banking. Banks can **store** more information, use **less** paper, and process transations more **quickly** and more cheaply. As a result, customers can check their **accounts**, pay bills and **withdraw** money without ever entering a bank.

14.4

a in the red. **b** tied up. **c** put on hold. **d** on the blink.

Unit 15: Making arrangements

15.1

1 Jakarta, Indonesia.
2 Before 8 May.
3 Business negotiations with Sunrise Products PTE.
4 The chairman and other key people in Sunrise Products PTE.
5 Hotel Borobodur Intercontinental.

15.2

1d. 2a. 3b. 4e. 5f. 6c. 7g. 8h.

15.4

BUSINESS TRAVEL LIMITED
Flight request form

Name of passenger (s) **Mr Ray SMITH**
Number of passengers: Adults: **1**   Children: **0**
Flying from **London** To **Jakarta**   Single or return **Return**
Date of travel **4 May 2001**
Date of return **13 May 2001**

Preferred airline **Emirates?**
Preferred route / stopovers **none**
Class: First / Business / Economy **business**

Hotel booking required? **Yes – Hotel Borobodur Intercontinental**

Car hire, pick up, other services **none**

15.6

1 None.
2 It was full.
3 Hilton Hotel.
4 **d** BTL will mail the ticket to Kate.
5 **d** BTL will send a bill to be paid later.

```
Ticket for Mr Ray Smith
Thursday 4th May   Depart London Heathrow Airport  Flight EMI 7721   12.30
                   Arrive Dubai International                         21.45
                   Depart Dubai International        Flight EMI 2190   23.00
Friday 5th May     Arrive Jakarta Soekarno-Hatta                      13.10
Saturday 13th May  Depart Jakarta Soekarno-Hatta    Flight EMI 2191   08.00
                   Arrive Dubai International                          14.05
                   Depart Dubai International        Flight EMI 7720   15.20
                   Arrive London Heathrow Airport                     20.00
Special meals:     normal meals / vegetarian / vegan / other (please specify)

Hotel Hilton International. 5th May – 13th May (8 nights).
Type of room:  single / double / suite
Invoice to:  International Plastics  Account Number IP23Z
Tickets:  courier / first class post / customer collects / pick up at airport
```

15.7

1 Ray Smith is going to Indonesia on 4 May.
2 His plane leaves from Heathrow Airport.
3 It takes off at 12.30.
4 He is staying there for eight nights.
5 He is staying in Hotel Hilton International.
6 On Monday 8 May, David Sitorus is showing him around Sunrise Products' plants.
7 He is meeting the chairman of Sunrise Products on Monday 8 May.
8 He is flying back to the UK on Saturday 13 May.
9 His flight arrives back in the UK at 8 p.m.
10 Someone from Sunrise Products is meeting him at the airport in Jakarta.

15.8

The meeting will be on Wednesday 3 May at 10.30 a.m.

15.9

A

1 It's too late. Ray Smith is leaving for Indonesia.

2 She is interviewing someone.
3 Helen has a meeting in Birmingham.
4 In France with his children – he has the day off.
5 An appointment with a software supplier
6 Probably in Ray Smith's office.

C 1b. 2e. 3h. 4d. 5a. 6c. 7f. 8g.

Unit 16: Meetings

16.2

A 1e. 2a. 3c. 4f. 5g. 6d. 7b.

B 1 circulate/agenda.
  2 items.
  3 minutes.
  4 apologies.

16.3

A 2, 3, 7, 8, 10, 11.

B Bringing forward the date for changes to hotel's software.

C The last time the company installed new software, it was a nightmare.

D *Atsushi and Carl send their apologies.*
  Minutes of last meeting.
  Security firm.
  New software.

16.4

1 Carl Reich was not present.
  Apologies for absence came from Carl Reich and Atsushi Morita.
2 New pay rates to start on 1st not 10th.
3 The first topic discussed was the implementation of new software *not* the date for new computers.
  It was Johann Elias, not AT, who assured the meeting that problems would be minimal – about two weeks.
  Person responsible is Johann Elias, not MG.
  The deadline is the start of next month, not the end.
4 The second topic concerns problems with security staff who have been rude and rather bossy.
  Action to be taken: Pablo Martinez will phone the company.
  AT are not the initials of anyone present at the meeting.
  No deadline was given for action on the second topic.

16.5

A 1h. 2g. 3f. 4e. 5d. 6c. 7a & b. 8a & b.
B 1 Can I come in here?
   2 What do you think?
   3 That's what I thought too.
   4 Well... I'm not exactly looking forward to it.
   5 When would the changes actually start?

16.6

Dubai – women should dress modestly. Dubai and Japan – business happens slowly, good personal relations are very important. France – people shake hands frequently. USA – people use first names more readily.

Unit 17: The changing job market

17.1

Some words are clearly and easily associated with temps or permanent workers. For example, temporary workers: flexibility, cheap labour, motivation, cost-cutting, casual labour; permanent workers: job security, company loyalty. However, others, e.g. stress, are a matter of opinion.

17.2

1 **a** is best but **b** is also possible.
2 *Possible Advantages*: workers less anxious; workers gain a broad range of skills and experience
   Possible Disadvantages: workers can easily lose their jobs; communication and understanding of company practices may not be so good with temporary staff; workers do not get the opportunity to develop themselves.

17.3

1b. 2b. 3c. 4a. 5a. 6b. 7c. 8a. 9c.

17.4

1 it = replace full-time staff with temps; they = temps; some = employers.
2 Keeping down payrolls.
3 temporary
4 **a** False (paragraph 1). **b** True (paragraph 3). **c** False (paragraph 4). **d** True (paragraph 6).
5 Because the disadvantages of outsourcing may be too great.

17.5

Paragraph 1: introduction
Paragraph 2: academic viewpoint
Paragraph 3: employer's viewpoint
Paragraph 4: employer's viewpoint
Paragraph 5: advantages of outsourcing
Paragraph 6: conclusion

17.7

make redundant / lay off / recession / lose / to fire / strike / to get the sack / let go / to get the axe.

17.8

1 Nine, including Yonhap News Agency.
2 South Korea's top companies present restructuring plans.

17.9

1b. 2a. 3b. 4b. 5a. 6b. 7b. 8c. 9b. 10a.

17.10

A 1c. 2c.

B 2 Samsung. 3 Hyundai, SK. 4 Daewoo.

17.11

2 competition, to compete, competitive, competitive advantage
3 transfer, to transfer, transferred, transfer funds
4 earnings, to earn, earned, earned income
5 register, to register, registered, registered company
6 highlight, to highlight, highlighted

Unit 18: Check your progress

18.1

```
From: Ray Smith <rsmith@mda.com>
To: David Sitorus <ho@sunrise-products.co.id>
Date: Thursday 29th April
Subject: trip to Indonesia
```

Dear David

I will be **arriving** in Jakarta at Soekarno-Hatta Airport at 13.10 on Friday 5th May. I'm **flying** with Emirates and my flight number is EMI 7721. Can you confirm that someone will be able to **pick** me up at the airport? By the way, I will not be staying at the Hotel Borobodur as it is completely **full**. I am booked into the Hilton Hotel.

We are also **sending** you some sample materials and some technical documents by courier. You should have those by Monday midday at the latest. Please let me **know** if they do not arrive. They **are** coming with Europe and Asia couriers and the reference number is JAK37274A.

I look **forward** to seeing you again next week. Let me know if there is **anything** you would **like** me to bring from London.

Regards

Ray Smith

18.2

Who is he flying with?
How much did it cost?
Where is he staying?
How long is he staying?
Who is he meeting?
How long is the flight?

18.3

Possible answers:

a How about tomorrow at 11 am?
b Excuse me, could you tell me how the photocopier works, please?
c May I use your phone to make a quick call to the office?
d I'm having trouble with my printer.
e I'm sorry. He's not here today. Can I take a message?
f Tomorrow at 11 will be fine.

18.4

1	trip	**8**	made
2	staying	**9**	permanent
3	flight (plane)	**10**	cut, reduce
4	arrange (organize, fix, fix up, set up)	**11**	on
5	free (available)	**12**	have
6	minutes	**13**	agree
7	shake	**14**	price (cost)

LANGUAGE REFERENCE

1 Tenses

	present	present perfect	past	past perfect
simple	Sales increase.	Sales have increased.	Sales increased.	Sales had increased.
continuous	Sales are increasing.	Sales have been increasing.	Sales were increasing.	Sales had been increasing.

future	Prices are going to increase. Prices will increase. Prices are falling from tomorrow.

Present simple

- You use this tense when talking about habitual actions (not a specific occasion) or when talking generally.

  Examples: She reads the *Financial Times* every morning.

  He visits the gym twice a week.

  Unilever employs about 290,000 people world-wide.

- You can use the present simple to discuss the future when talking about programmes and timetables.

  Examples: The plane leaves at 4.30 pm on Wednesday.

  The courses start next month.

Present continuous

■ You use this tense to talk about actions that are not finished or that someone is still in the process of doing.

Examples: Faisal is working in the marketing department till the end of August.

I'm still reading that report on the new marketing plan.

■ You can use the present continuous to talk about future arrangements.

Examples: The company is opening another plant in La Paz in February next year.

■ Some verbs are not usually used in the present continuous form.

Examples:	verbs of thinking:	*know realise remember forget*
	verbs of feeling or emotions:	*like hate want prefer*
	verbs of the senses:	*hear see smell*
	verbs of possession:	*belong own possess*

Present perfect

We use the present perfect when talking about an action which in some way connects the present to the past.

■ It is used to talk about something that began in the past and continues in the present.

Example: He has worked in the Barcelona office since May 2000.
(i.e. *He began in May 2000 and is still working there.*)

■ It is used when talking about something that happened at an unspecified time in the past and which has a result in the present.

Example: Oh no! I've left my diary at home. (*Result: I do not have my diary now.*)

for and *since*

We use *for* to describe the length of an action and *since* to indicate when it started.

Examples: I have known Ryuichi *for 8* years.

I have known Ryuichi *since* 1996.

just, yet and *already*

These words are often used with the present perfect.

Examples: John has *just* left the building.

Have you spoken to Pierre *yet?*

Martha has *already* gone home.

NB One of the small differences between British and American English concerns the use of the present perfect. Americans often use the simple past with *just/yet/already* instead of the present perfect.

British English	**American English**
John has just left the building.	John just left the building.
Have you spoken to Pierre yet?	Did you speak to Pierre yet?
Martha has already gone home.	Martha went home already.

Simple past

We use this tense to refer to a completed action in the past.

> **Examples:** The price of ICI shares rose by 10% last year.
> Did you go to the meeting yesterday?

Past continuous

This tense is used to talk about an action in the past that we were in the middle of doing.

> **Example:** When we met her last year, I was still training to become an accountant.

Past perfect

This tense is used to talk about past events that occurred before other past events.

> **Examples:** After they had finished the project, they went home.
> It had been a difficult time. The company had reorganized and in the process many jobs had been lost.

NB The past perfect is often used in reported speech.

> **Examples:** She phoned yesterday. → She said that she had phoned yesterday.
> Profits rose sharply. → The newspaper reported that profits had risen sharply.

Past perfect continuous

This tense is used to talk about an action that happened over a period of time and continued up to a certain time in the past.

> **Example:** The business had been doing very well until the winter of 2000.

Compare the present perfect continuous and the past perfect continuous:

> He looks tired. He has been working late again.
> He looked tired. He had been working late again.

Future

As well as *will* we can use *going to* and the present continuous to express future meaning.

■ We can use *will* when making predictions or general statements about the future.
   Example: By the end of the year 2003, the population of Britain will be about 61 million.

■ We can use the present continuous to talk about future arrangements.
   Example: We're meeting at 6 pm this evening.

■ We can use *going to* + infinitive to emphasize intentions.
   Example: I'm going to discuss the problem with him at the first opportunity tomorrow morning.

2 Modals

I You He She We They	can may might must ought to should	check the share price every day. book the tickets on the Internet.

Modals are used often in English and express a large variety of ideas, such as ability, possibility, certainty, permission and obligation.
Remember:

■ Whether we use *I*, *you*, *we*, *he*, *she* or *they*, the form of the modal verb does not change.
   Examples: Abdulah was ill on Wednesday so he couldn't come to the meeting.
   Company employees can purchase goods at a 10% discount.

■ *do/does* are not used in questions or in negatives.
   Examples: May I speak to the manager, please?
   You must not smoke anywhere inside the building.

■ Most modals (except *ought to*) are followed by the infinitive without *to*.
Examples: He looks ill. He should go to the doctor.

You ought to ask Charles Guilbert in the Finance department for advice on this matter.

3 *If...* sentences

Examples: If you pay by cash, you'll get a 5% discount on your purchase.

If the government raised company taxes, it would probably result in higher unemployment.

If I had known that, I wouldn't have signed the contract.

These sentences consist of an *if*-clause (*If you pay by cash*) and a main clause *(you'll get a 5% discount on your purchase)*. There are a number of possible combinations of verb forms. The most common are:

■ **Type 1**

Form: *If* + present simple, *will*

We use the first type to talk about the results of something that may happen in the future.

Example: If you post the parcel this afternoon, it will arrive tomorrow morning.

■ **Type 2**

Form: *If* + past, *would*

We use the second type to talk about something that probably won't happen.

Example: If I won the lottery, I would buy a boat and sail around the world.

■ **Type 3**

Form: *If* + past perfect, *would have*

We use the third type to talk about something that is an impossibility now.

Example: If the employers had not agreed to a pay rise, the transport workers would have gone on strike.

4 Passive

Active: *Information technology has radically changed the way many industries work.*

Passive: *The way many industries work has been radically changed by information technology.*

Active: *Mr Ling will lead the project team.*

Passive: *The project team will be led by Mr Ling.*

In these sentences, the meaning is the same but the emphasis is different. In the active sentences, the emphasis is on the thing (or person) doing the action. In the passive sentences, the emphasis is on the thing (or person) affected by the action. The passive is often used in formal written language to achieve an impersonal tone.

Form: subject + *to be* + past participle

Examples:

Present simple

Most of the components are imported from Taiwan.

Present continuous

A new office block is being built in the suburbs.

Present perfect

The ship has not been badly damaged.

Simple past

Chambers Ltd, an electrical goods company, was established in 1950 by Peter Chambers.

Past continuous

Your report was being read by Martin when I arrived at the office.

Past perfect

The parcel had been delivered by courier while I was out of the office.

Will and other modal verbs (*can, could, ought t*o, etc.) use *be* + the past participle:

The goods will be sent to you by courier next Monday.

Purchases can be paid in cash or by credit card.

5 Relative clauses

	defining		non-defining	
	people	**things**	**people**	**things**
subject	who, that	which, that	who	which
object	who, that, *whom	which, that	who, *whom	which
possessive	whose	whose	whose	whose

*Used in formal writing but is now considered old-fashioned and is not often used in speech or informal writing.

There are two types of relative clause: the defining relative clause and the non-defining relative clause.

i The defining relative clause provides essential information and tells us exactly which person or thing is being referred to.

Examples: The company which produced these components has closed down.

Employers who treat their employees fairly are always respected.

NB Commas are not used to separate the relative clause and the main clause. It is possible to leave out *who, that* or *which* when they are the object of a relative clause, e.g. Some of the people (that) we met at the exhibition were very interested in our product.

ii The non-defining relative clause provides extra, non-essential information.

Examples: Anita Roddick, who started the Body Shop organisation about 25 years ago, has written a new book on her approach to business.

Maria Carlucci, who runs the fashion department, is on vacation at the moment.

NB Commas are usually used to separate the relative clause and the main clause. *That* is not used in non-defining relative clauses.

6 Reported speech

Direct speech: "I haven't seen Melissa for ages."
Reported speech: He said he hadn't seen Melissa for ages.

In moving from direct to reported speech certain changes may occur. If the reporting verb is in the past (e.g. *asked, said*), then usually the verb in the reported clause moves one step further back in the past. Thus,

present → past
present perfect → past perfect
past → past perfect

However, if the reporting verb is in the present, then the tense in the reported clause needn't be changed:
Direct speech: *"Oil prices are rising"*
Reported speech: *He says that oil prices are rising.*

7 Articles: *the, a/an*

Some of the most common uses of *the* are:

- when talking about something / someone that is unique, e.g. *the president of Mexico, the* Wall Street Journal, *the best swimmer in the world*

- when talking about a particular person / thing or when it is obvious who / what is meant, e.g. *I spoke to the manager earlier today. She said the office closes at 5 pm.*

- hotels, e.g. *the Hilton*

Some of the most common uses of *a / an* are:

- when referring to a single thing, e.g. *Could you recommend a good hotel in Lima?*

- when referring to a job, e.g. *She's a teacher. He's an accountant.*

No article

We do not use *the* or *a / an*:

- when making generalizations referring to plural nouns (e.g. *Computers are expensive to buy.*) or uncountable nouns (e.g. *Everybody needs money.*)

- with most proper nouns (names), e.g. *Faisal Ali, Maria Gonzalez*

8 Phrasal verbs

Examples:
I've been *looking for* another job.
Please *switch off* all the computers before you leave.
The missing documents *turned up* two days later.

A phrasal verb is a combination of a verb (*look, make, put, switch, cut,* etc.) with one or two particles (adverbs or prepositions such as *on, off, away, forward, to* etc.).

Sometimes the meaning of the verb can be guessed easily if you know the meaning of its parts:
He *got off* the plane.
Please *take* your coat *off.*

More often though, phrasal verbs are idioms. You can't easily guess the meaning of the whole expression just by knowing what its parts mean.
The plane *took off.*
I'm really *looking forward* to my holiday
She left the job because she couldn't *get on with* her boss.

In terms of grammar there are three groups of phrasal verbs:

i Intransitive verbs. These have no object and the adverb always comes directly after the verb.

Examples:
The plane *took off.*
The meeting *went on* for hours.
The number of customers has *fallen off* recently.

ii Transitive inseparable verbs. The preposition in these verbs always comes after the verb and before the object (even if the object is a preposition).

Examples:
He wasn't looking forward to the meeting.
He wasn't looking forward to it.

iii Transitive separable verbs. The particle in these phrasal verbs can come before or after the object.

Examples:
Don't forget to *turn* the computer *off* before you leave.
Don't forget to *turn off* the computer before you leave.

He *gave up* his job last month.
He *gave* his job *up* last month.

If the object is a pronoun (such as *it, them, you, this, him, her, us*), the particle must follow the pronoun, it can't come before it:

He didn't like his job so he *gave* it *up*.
Can you check the computers, please? I'm not sure if I *turned* them *off*.

Note that some phrasal verbs can be both transitive and intransitive, with different meanings:

The plane *took off* an hour late. (*intransitive*)
She *took* her coat *off*. (*transitive, separable*)

Here are some common *intransitive* phrasal verbs:

take off	My plane takes off at 13.45.
check in	You must check in at least 2 hours before departure.
go on	The meeting went on for over 3 hours.
drop off	Profits have dropped off sharply in the last 6 months.
break down	Sorry I'm late. My car broke down.

Here are some common *inseparable* phrasal verbs:

look forward to	I'm really looking forward to my holiday.
run into	I ran into an old friend of yours at a conference last week.
get on with	Can we get on with the meeting? I have to leave by 5 today.
take care of	There was a problem with the fax machine but the technician took care of it.
look after	Jane Myers, the personnel manager, looks after all issues related to staff training and promotion.
carry on with	Let's have lunch now and then we can carry on with our discussions afterwards.

Here are some common *separable* phrasal verbs:

switch on	It's better to switch the monitor on before the PC.
switch off	If you switch the lights off, we will be able to see the presentation more clearly.
turn on	Turn on the answerphone before you leave the office.
turn off	It has been estimated that turning off all the computers in the office at night could save us $10,000 a year.
set up	Can you set up a meeting with David and Sally for some time next week?

take over	There had been rumours that Sabena would be taken over by Virgin Atlantic Airlines.
put off	We'll have to put off the meeting until next month because Juan has gone into hospital.

9 Verb + ing or verb + to + infinitive?

You will often hear or read sentences where one verb is followed by another verb.

Sometimes the second verb will take an *-ing* form and sometimes it will take the form of *to + infinitive*.

Examples:

He *risked losing* a lot of money if the plan had failed.

She *mentioned seeing* him at the trade fair in Leipzig last month.

We *agreed to meet* again in two weeks' time.

The management *wanted to introduce* new pay scales for the employees.

Verbs usually followed by the *-ing* form include:

admit	appreciate	resist	can't help
delay	deny	dislike	can't stand
finish	practise	stop	miss
suggest			

Verbs usually followed by *to + infinitive* include:

agree	ask	can't afford	choose
decide	expect	neglect	happen
hope	manage	promise	plan
refuse	seem	want	would like

Some verbs (for example, *begin, hate, like, prefer, start, continue, intend*) can be followed by either the *-ing* form or *to + infinitive* and often there is no great difference in meaning:

Examples:

He began working at 9 am and didn't finish till 2 pm.

He began to work at 9 am and didn't finish till 2 pm.

I like watching football on the television.

I like to watch football on the television.

Pronunciation

Phonemic symbols

A good English dictionary can help with understanding pronunciation. This is especially important if you are teaching yourself. It is very helpful therefore to be able to use the phonemic alphabet – these are symbols used in dictionaries to explain the pronunciation of words.

Vowels and dipthongs

ɪ	sit	/ sɪt /		ɪə	ear	/ ɪə /
i:	see	/ si: /		eɪ	page	/ peɪdʒ /
ʊ	look	/ lʊk /		ʊə	pure	/ pjʊə /
u:	two	/ tu: /		ɔɪ	boy	/ bɔɪ /
e	egg	/ eg /		əʊ	no	/ nəʊ /
ə	about	/ əbaʊt /		eə	there	/ ðeə /
ɜ:	learn	/ lɜ:n /		aɪ	eye	/ aɪ /
ɔ:	short	/ ʃɔ:t /		aʊ	now	/ naʊ /
æ	hat	/ hæt /				
ʌ	cup	/ kʌp /				
ɑ:	arm	/ ɑ:m /				
ɒ	got	/ gɒt /				

Consonants

p	pen	/ pen /		s	so	/ səʊ /
b	bee	/ bi: /		z	zoo	/ zu: /
t	tea	/ ti: /		ʃ	she	/ ʃi: /
d	dog	/ dɒg /		ʒ	pleasure	/ pleʒə /
k	cat	/ kæt /		h	house	/ haʊs /
g	got	/ gɒt /		m	me	/ mi: /
tʃ	chair	/ tʃeə /		n	no	/ nəʊ /
dʒ	just	/ dʒʌst /		ŋ	long	/ lɒŋ /
f	five	/ faɪv /		l	leg	/ leg /
v	very	/ verɪ /		r	right	/ raɪt /
θ	thin	/ θɪn /		j	yes	/ jes /
ð	this	/ ðɪs /		w	we	/ wi: /

Stress

When we speak, the emphasis we give to a particular part of a word is called **stress**. For example, the stress in *number* is on the first syllable. In the word *advise*, it is on the second syllable.

Dictionaries usually indicate the pronunciation of a word using phonemic symbols, e.g. *computer* /kəmpju:tə/. However, if you do not know phonemic symbols, you can still work out the stress. Normally, there is a ' symbol before the stressed part, e.g. *number* /'nʌmbə/, *advise* /əd'vaɪz/.

TAKING IT FURTHER

Useful Web Addresses

Dictionaries

1 British English dictionary
   http://www.cup.cam.ac.uk/elt/dictionary
2 American English dictionary
   http://www.merriam.webster.com
3 A dictionary of financial vocabulary
   http://Investorwords.com

Newspapers, magazines and news organizations

4 *The Financial Times* newspaper
   http://www.ft.com
5 *The Economist*
   http://www.economist.com
6 *The Wall Street Journal*
   http://www.wsj.com
7 *Business Week*
   http://www.businessweek.com
8 *Fortune* magazine
   http://www.fortune.com
   The website of *Fortune* magazine produces interesting lists, such as the "America's most admired companies", "the 100 fastest growing companies", "the most powerful women".
9 *BBC Business news*
   http://www.bbc.co.uk/worldservice/business/index.shtml
   World business news to read or listen to.

10 Netscape Business news
http://dailynews.netscape.com/dailynews/business/main.tmpl

Learning English – General English and Business English Sites

11 BBC learning English
http://www.bbc.uk/worldservice/features/learningenglish/index.shtml
Includes learning Business English
http://www.bbc.co.uk/worldservice/learningenglish/work/index.shtml

12 The British Council
http://www.britishcoun.org/english

13 Dave Sperling's ESL café. Lots of useful pages for all aspects of learning English and links to many other sites
http://www.eslcafe.com/
Includes resources for learning business English
http://www.eslcafe.com/search/Business_English/

Other useful websites

Sites with links to business information
14 http://www.niss.ac.uk/cr/business.html
15 http://personal.dis.strath.ac.uk/business/

Job search sites. You can read job advertisements and also view CVs of people looking for new jobs
16 http://www.SuperJobSearch.com/html/profiles.html
17 http://www.SuperStaff.com/WentworthJL/Wentworth1.html
18 http://www.elmundo.es/empleo/

Sites which look at differences between British English and American English
19 http://www.scit.wlv.ac.uk/~jphb/american.html

Help with writing business letters, job applications and CVs
20 http://www.ruthvilmi.net/hut/help/writing_instructions/
21 http://www.swin.edu.au/corporate/careers/coverletter.htm
22 http://owl.english.purdue.edu/handouts/pw/
23 http://www1.umn.edu/ohr/ecep/resume/

Learning the skills and language needed for business meetings
24 http://www.stir.ac.uk/departments/humansciences/celt/staff/higdox/
Vallance/Diss/fp.htm

Tips and advice for job interviews, presentations and other communication skills
25 http://www.mapnp.org/library/commskls/cmm_face.htm

Tips for visitors to the UK including cultural information. Intended for visitors from the USA but useful for anyone
26 http://www.london-daily.co.uk/guide/gd-tips.htm

INDEX

Other related titles

 TEACH YOURSELF

AMERICAN ENGLISH

Sandra Stevens

If you know some English already and want to learn more without a teacher, this book is for you. *Teach Yourself American English* is easy to use and will give you the confidence to communicate in everyday situations. The course contains:

- clear and simple explanations
- interesting examples and exercises
- lots of practice in communication, grammar, vocabulary and pronunciation
- special sections which answer common questions and help you avoid making mistakes
- revision tests for you to check your progress

Teach Yourself American English will help you to improve quickly and without a teacher.

Other related titles

ENGLISH

Sandra Stevens

If you know some English already and want to learn more without a teacher, this book is for you. *Teach Yourself English* is easy to use and will give you the confidence to communicate in everyday situations. The course contains:

- clear and simple explanations
- interesting examples and exercises
- lots of practice in communication, grammar, vocabulary and pronunciation
- special sections which answer common questions and help you avoid making mistakes
- revision tests for you to check your progress
- information about British life and customs

Teach Yourself English will help you to improve quickly and without a teacher.

Other related titles

 TEACH YOURSELF

ENGLISH GRAMMAR

John Shepheard

Teach Yourself English Grammar helps you to learn and understand English grammar without a teacher. It makes learning English grammar easy and enjoyable, because it:

- gives you tips on how to learn the rules
- presents the grammar in clear and interesting situations
- shows you the common mistakes students make
- gives you practice in choosing the correct forms and making sentences
- helps you to write about yourself and your own life
- has the answers to all the exercises at the back of the book

Coming soon

ENGLISH LANGUAGE, LIFE & CULTURE

**Anne Fraenkel, Richard Haill &
Seamus O'Riordan**

Are fish and chips really the favourite food of the English?
Who were the Suffragettes?
What is the difference between England and Britain?
What is Elton John's real name?

This book answers these questions, and many more, in a concise and lively overview of England: the country, its heritage and its people. Vocabulary lists and 'Taking it Further' sections at the end of each unit give the student and the enthusiastic traveller the means to talk and write confidently about all aspects of English life.

The book looks at: government, arts, language, work, leisure, education, festivals, food – and much more besides! This is your key to understanding England's past, present and future, with plenty of suggestions for further study and background reading.